New Zealand and the British Empire: The History of British Sovereignty

By Charles River Editors

A mid-19th century painting of a Scottish Highland family in New Zealand

About Charles River Editors

Charles River Editors is a boutique digital publishing company, specializing in bringing history back to life with educational and engaging books on a wide range of topics. Keep up to date with our new and free offerings with this 5 second sign up on our weekly mailing list, and visit Our Kindle Author Page to see other recently published Kindle titles.

We make these books for you and always want to know our readers' opinions, so we encourage you to leave reviews and look forward to publishing new and exciting titles each week.

Introduction

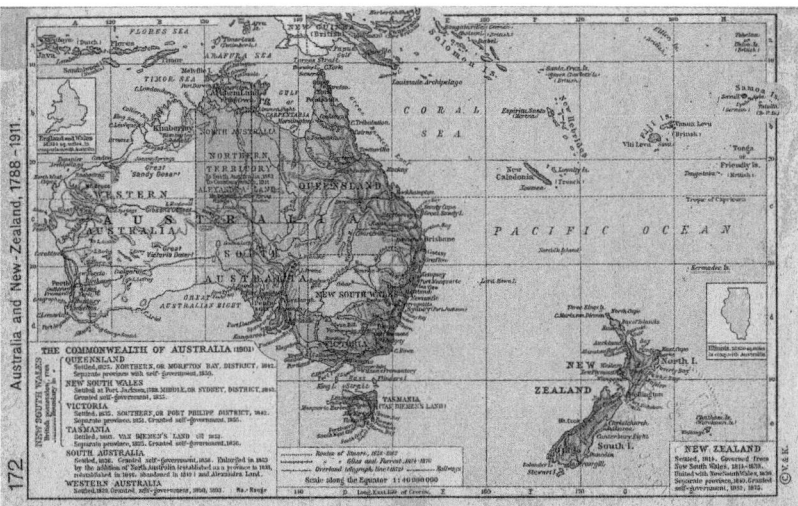

New Zealand and the British Empire

"When one house dies, a second lives." - Māori proverb

By the mid-17th century, the existence of a land in the south referred to as Terra Australis was generally known and understood by the Europeans, and incrementally, its shores were observed and mapped. Van Diemen's Land, an island off the south coast of Australia now called Tasmania, was identified in 1642 by Dutch mariner Abel Tasman, and a few months later, the intrepid Dutchman would add New Zealand to the map of the known world.

At the time, the English were the greatest naval power in Europe, but they arrived on the scene rather later. The first to appear was William Dampier, captain of the HMS Roebuck, in 1699, after he had been granted a Royal Commission by King William III to explore the east coast of New Holland. By then, the general global balance of power was shifting, and with the English gaining a solid foothold in India, their supremacy in the Indian Ocean trade zone began. The Dutch, once predominant in the region, began slowly to lose ground, slipping out of contention as a major global trading power. So too were the Portuguese, also once dominant in the region. It was now just the French and the English who were facing one another down in a quest to dominate the world, but their imperial interests were focused mainly in India and the East Indies, as well as the Caribbean and the Americas. As a result, the potential of a vast, practically uninhabited great southern continent did not yet hold much interest.

By then the world was largely mapped, with just regions such as the Arctic Archipelago and the two poles remaining terra incognita. A few gaps needed to be filled in here and there, but all of the essential details were known. At the same time, a great deal of imperial energy was at play in Europe, particularly in Britain. Britain stood at the cusp of global dominance thanks almost entirely to the Royal Navy, which emerged in the 17th and 18th centuries as an institution significantly more than the sum of its parts. With vast assets available even in peacetime, expeditions of science and explorations were launched in every direction. This was done not only to claim ownership of the field of global exploration, but also to undercut the imperial ambitions of others, in particular the French.

In 1769, Captain James Cook's historic expedition in the region would lead to an English claim on Australia, but before he reached Australia, he sailed near New Zealand and spent weeks mapping part of New Zealand's coast. Cook later asserted that the only major sources of timber and flax in the Pacific region were to be found in New Zealand and Norfolk Island, which would prove crucial to the British Empire and the Royal Navy in particular, and Cook also provided a firsthand account of a tense standoff with New Zealand's indigenous natives on the shoreline. Over the next 90 years, Cook's journey and his account would lay the basis for British activities in the region, and those activities would forge the modern history of New Zealand at a great cost.

New Zealand and the British Empire: The History of New Zealand under British Sovereignty analyzes the expeditions that discovered New Zealand, the early settlements and conflicts waged there from 1650-1850, and the exploration that mapped New Zealand and led to its status as a dominion. Along with pictures of important people, places, and events, you will learn about New Zealand under British sovereignty like never before.

New Zealand and the British Empire: The History of New Zealand under British Sovereignty
About Charles River Editors
Introduction
   New Zealand's First Arrivals
   The Musket Wars
   Missionaries and Whalers
   The Founding of a Colony
   Immigration and Settlement
   The Exploration of New Zealand's Interior
   The New Zealand Wars
   The Economics of Settlement
   The Social Landscape
   New Zealand at War
   New Zealand as a Dominion
   Appendix: The Treaty of Waitangi
   Online Resources
   Bibliography
Free Books by Charles River Editors
Discounted Books by Charles River Editors

New Zealand's First Arrivals

On December 13, 1642, a Dutch survey expedition led by Abel Tasman and comprised of two ships, *Heemskerck* and *Zeehaen*, encountered in the South Pacific what Tasman later described as "a large land uplifted high." What Tasman was in fact looking at was the South Island of New Zealand, and the uplifted high land consisted of the Southern Alps. This land Tasman declared "*Staten Landt*," or "State Land," and a few days later the small flotilla drifted into Cook Strait.[1] There the two ships anchored in a natural harbor now known as "*Mohua*," or as it is known today, Golden Bay. There Tasman found a deeply indented shoreline and calm waters, fringed by wooded hills, and gifted with a mild and temperate climate. It certainly was a pleasing sight, and Tasman earmarked it as a country perfectly suited to future European settlement.

A contemporary portrait believed to depict Tasman and his family

Then, quite unexpectedly, this utopian aspect was shattered when a flotilla of war canoes detached itself from shore and rushed out to meet them. A brief skirmish followed, and a few Dutch sailors were killed before a round of shots was fired that immediately dispersed the

---

[1] There are different versions of this naming. Another is that Tasman believed it to be connected to Argentina's Staten Island, or *Isla de los Estados*.

attackers. The sides separated and the natives returned to shore. They had never encountered ballistics before, so the experience undoubtedly scared them, but Tasman quickly hoisted sail and hurried back to open water. He later wrote of the encounter, "In the evening about one hour after sunset we saw many lights on land and four vessels near the shore, two of which betook themselves towards us. When our two boats returned to the ships reporting that they had found not less than thirteen fathoms of water, and with the sinking of the sun (which sank behind the high land) they had been still about half a mile from the shore. After our people had been on board about one glass, people in the two canoes began to call out to us in gruff, hollow voices. We could not in the least understand any of it; however, when they called out again several times we called back to them as a token answer. But they did not come nearer than a stone's shot. They also blew many times on an instrument, which produced a sound like the moors' trumpets. We had one of our sailors (who could play somewhat on the trumpet) play some tunes to them in answer."

Tasman named the place Murderer's Bay and continued on, arriving next in the Tongan Archipelago. To the Dutch captain, who had already touched the shores of *Terra Australis*, or "New Holland" as he left it, this first encounter with the natives of New Zealand was sobering. The Australian Aboriginals he had previously met were either friendly or semi-wild, fleeing to the bush like hares at the first sight of a white man. He had certainly never expected to be met on shore by a war party, and he immediately understood that anyone attempting to conquer and settle this land would certainly need to be prepared to fight for it.

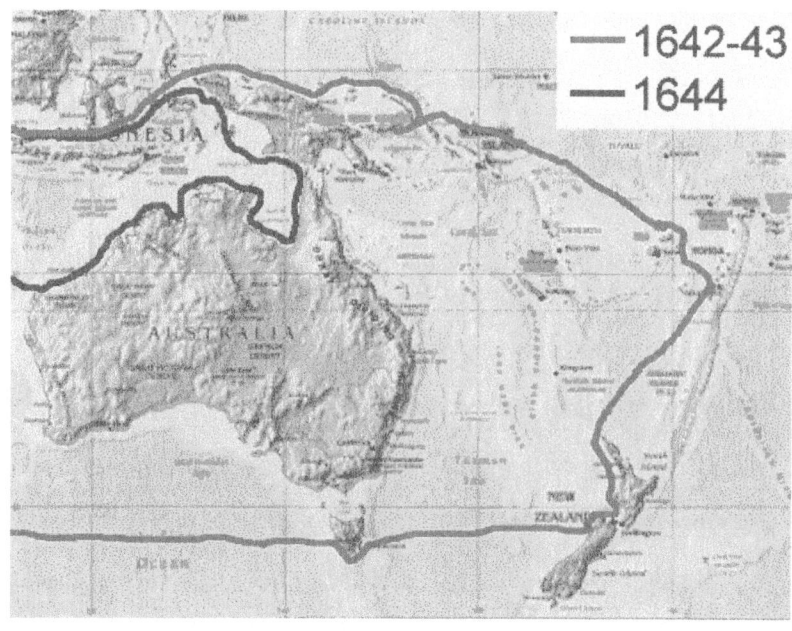

A map of Tasman's voyages in the region

A contemporary depiction of Murderer's Bay

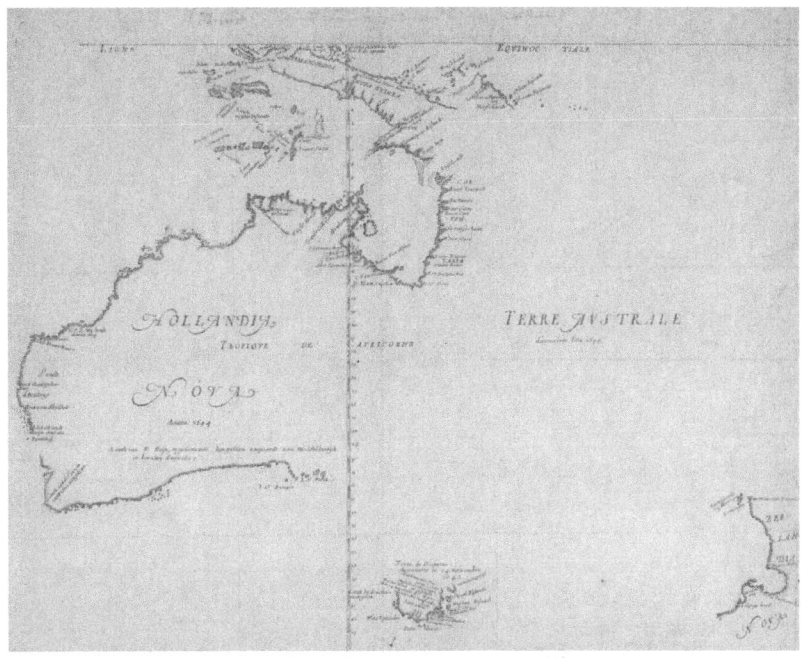

A 1645 map of the region

Archeologists have since explained this initial encounter as the unexpected arrival of an entirely unknown race into an area of settlement and agriculture, and the natural impulse that the indigenous people would feel to protect it. Nonetheless, this first European encounter with the Māori must certainly have presented a striking and intimidating picture. Warlike and tribal, the Māori were then, as they are now, flamboyant and decorative, fond of rituals and ceremonies, and accustomed to warfare as a cultural expression and means of inhabiting an accommodating land. Their distinctive tattoos, both erotic and totemic, were unique and striking expressions of a robust and violent, but also deeply accomplished society.

A 19th century depiction of Māoris

Historians can still only estimate when the first people reached Australia, but Māoris are known to have begun making landfall in New Zealand less than 1,000 years ago, around the early 14th century. According to local lore, "Kupe," the first Polynesian mariner to arrive on New Zealand's shores, is typically described today as an "explorer," which implies a systematic search for new lands. Kupe's home, however, was the island of "Hawaiki," a mythical island from where the Polynesian race originated, and these origins tend to flavor Kupe's odyssey with the elements of a genesis story. Nonetheless, it was at about that time the Polynesians began to settle on New Zealand. Riding the currents of the South Pacific Gyre, and following the stars, the first arrivals came across more than 2,600 miles of ocean in large ocean-going canoes known as *waka*. The origins of this migration are somewhere in the region of French Polynesia, Tahiti, and the Cook and Society Islands. Currents and wind patterns deposited them eventually on North Island, from which there was little hope of return. Others soon followed, and as the generations progressed, a settled community took root.

There are a number of theories in regards to the style and pattern of this migration, but in essence the two main hypotheses suggest either a piecemeal movement or a single, "Great Fleet." Generally, it is the latter that is the more popular theory. This, of course, implies, at the very least, the confidence and skill of an accomplished maritime people, strong leadership, and a firm objective.

The Polynesians can trace their origins to south Asia, migrating over thousands of years from the coast and islands of China, along the Malay Archipelago, and across the South Pacific in an arc that would inevitably deposit them on the islands of New Zealand.[2] According to the "Great Fleet" theory, an expedition of at least seven canoes, carrying several hundred crew and passengers, was inspired by the reports of Kupe, and later the Polynesian explorers Toi and Whātonga, with the first substantial landfall taking place within a few years of 1280. A more ancient, nomadic people called *Moriori* were already present on North Island, but they were quickly wiped out by this invasion of aggressive and warlike Polynesians, who called themselves "Māori," or the "First People."[3]

This is the orthodox version of how the Māori came to be present in New Zealand, and if Abel Tasman had been granted the opportunity to look more closely at Māori society, what he would have found would have been an advanced, organized and adaptable people, warlike in disposition but agricultural. This was fortunate, because the incoming Māori found themselves stranded on a landscape and climate very different from that which they were accustomed. It required sturdier homes, more comprehensive clothing, and styles of agriculture more appropriate to a temperate climate. This process of adaption took time, but it was made quite a lot easier by the sheer bounty of the land, which had shorelines teeming with fish and interior landscapes populated by game. The first settlements congregated in the estuaries and around the river mouths of North Island, and the great flightless bird, the Moa, was an easy prey to hunt and could be found all over the place. Although hunted to extinction before the year 1500, the Moa nonetheless offered the Māori a vital bridge to the development of local agriculture.

As the centuries passed, the Māori gradually dispersed across both islands, slowly evolving their unique lifestyle and culture. As many Europeans would observe, however, a significant part of that culture revolved around warfare. Clans and tribes (*iwi*) began to separate, and soon enough they were at odds with one another. Before long, a revolving tradition of war took root, and from this tradition a "god of war" emerged, variously named *Tūmatauenga, Kahukura, Uenuku*, and *Maru*. The causes of war were often based on land and natural resources, but also based on revenge, slaves and sometimes tradition. A word – *"mana"* – evolved, which, in idiomatic terms, means something akin to spirituality, the "kismet" of victory and power. This ideology elevated warfare to something higher than the usual temporal pursuits of land, slaves and grievances, and towards something almost on the level of a religion.

On a practical, day-to-day level, Māori culture, although Stone Age, was nonetheless highly developed, especially in comparison to the Aboriginal communities of neighboring Australia. The Māori were of Polynesian origin, and their cultural peculiarities have tended to reflect that.

---

[2] The current theory, based on mitochondrial DNA, is that the Māori can trace their ancient origins to Taiwanese aboriginals some 5,200 years ago.

[3] Fresh archaeological evidence now suggests that the Moriori were a subgroup of mainland Māori, who migrated from New Zealand to the Chatham Islands, there developing their own distinctive, peaceful culture. This again is a contested theory.

Many of their implements were made of stone, at least partly, but the preferred materials were wood, ivory and bone. Everything from bird to whale bones, and indeed human bones, were used in constructing items as diverse as hoes, needles, and war clubs. Many types of hardwood were to be found on the island, and weapons of war were often wooden. It was a society rich in totems, and the varied depiction of these laid the foundation of a strong artistic tradition, featuring wood carving, body decoration, theater and oratory, and multiple rituals and ceremonies. Māori architecture was artistic, and reasonably advanced, while society was generally patrilineal, and the strongest political unit was the iwi.

A 19th century portrait of a Māori

Within a century or two of their arrival, the rival clans and iwi began to consolidate, confederate, and establish recognized and understood boundaries. The cult of warfare, thereafter, settled into a pattern not dissimilar to the great European estates of the Middle Ages. There was constant jostling for influence and authority, and a great deal of posturing and ceremony began to surround the business of war, which in due course became largely ceremonial itself.

A multilateral balance of power thus settled on the land, and a balanced social order was maintained, based on land and natural resources.

All of this, however, was shattered when the first substantive contact with European explorers took place.

The Musket Wars

"I have always found them of a brave, noble, open and benevolent disposition, but they are a people that will never put up with an insult if they have an opportunity to resent it." – Captain James Cook

Abel Tasman has long been considered the first European to make contact with New Zealand and its people, but new scholarship has theorized that the first European encounter with New Zealand took place over a century earlier by the Portuguese. It was in the year 1498 that the first Portuguese flotilla arrived on the coast of India, seeding Portuguese settlements along the coasts of India and East Africa. It has since been discovered that a great many of the fundamental achievements in exploration attributed to British, and other European explorers, were in fact preceded by Portuguese travelers and explorers. In this instance, the basis of the theory is simply that Portuguese exploradores were simple and illiterate men, and many of their early feats of exploration were never recorded. It is also true that they explored the trade in slaves, and thus they courted anonymity. Quite often, Portuguese travelers and commercial explorers were simply Portuguese speaking natives or half-castes, and their work also tended to be disregarded.

The notion, therefore, of Portuguese ships making first landfall in Australia and New Zealand is not entirely outlandish. Upon rounding the southern tip of the Indian subcontinent, and crossing the Bay of Bengal, the Malay Archipelago forms a natural conduit in the direction of Australia. The Portuguese founded numerous settlements in these regions, most notably Timor, located just a few hundred miles across the Sea of Timor to the coast of Western Australia. There is also strong material evidence that the Portuguese were aware of the existence of *Terra Australis*, in particular in reference to the "Dieppe Maps," a series of sixteenth century French world maps that portray the "Java la Grande" as corresponding to the northwest coast of Australia and scattered with Gallicized Portuguese place names. Artifacts thought to be of Portuguese origin have also been unearthed in adjacent coastal regions, and so the theory of prior Portuguese discovery of Australia, if not New Zealand, carries water. It is certainly not a great leap of imagination then to suppose that Portuguese ships, having come this far, might cross the Tasman Sea and set eyes on New Zealand.

Curiously, evidence of very early Spanish visits to New Zealand is a little bit stronger. In the northern Spanish city of La Coruna, a "pohutukawa" tree, native only to New Zealand, can be found. This specimen is estimated to be between 400 and 500 years old, and it is hard to imagine how a tree like that reached the Spanish coast unless a Spanish ship had collected it.

Either way, the first map to feature the name *Nova Zeelandia* was published by the Dutch in 1645, and no substantive European effort was made to exploit or visit this territory until at least a century later. After Abel Tasman, the next recorded European visit would be that of Captain James Cook.

In 1767, the Royal Society persuaded King George III to allocate funds for it to send an astronomer to the Pacific, and on January 1, 1768, the London Annual Register reported, "Mr. Banks, Dr. Solander, and Mr. Green the astronomer, set out for Deal, to embark on board the Endeavour, Captain Cook, for the South Seas, under the direction of the royal society, to observe the transit of Venus next summer, and to make discoveries." Mr. Banks was Joseph Banks, a botanist, and he brought along Dr. Daniel Solander, a Swedish naturalist. Charles Green was at that time the assistant to Nevil Maskelyne, the Astronomer Royal. The expedition, which would leave later in 1768, would be captained by Cook, a war veteran who had recently fought in the French & Indian War against the French in North America.

King George III

Banks

Solander

What the article did not mention was that the Admiralty was also hoping to find the famed Terra Australis Incognita, the legendary "unknown southern land." This came out later, when the *London Gazetteer* reported on August 18, 1768, "The gentlemen, who are to sail in a few days for George's Land, the new discovered island in the Pacific ocean, with an intention to observe the Transit of Venus, are likewise, we are credibly informed, to attempt some new discoveries in that vast unknown tract, above the latitude 40."

When Cook's expedition began in 1768, it included more than 80 men, consisting of 73 sailors and 12 members of the Royal Marines. Presumably, the expedition was supposed to be for entirely scientific – and hence peaceful – purposes. The *Endeavour* left Plymouth on August 26, 1768, and Cook landed at Matavai Bay, Tahiti, on April 13, 1769. The most important task at hand, other than day-to-day survival, was preparing to observe the transit of Venus that would occur on June 3.

Having completed the scientific assignments, the *Endeavour* next set sail in search of Terra Australis. After sailing for nearly two months, the crew earned the prize of being only the second group of Europeans to ever visit New Zealand. They arrived on October 6, 1769, and Cook described a harrowing experience when the men came ashore: "MONDAY, 9th October. ...I went ashore with a Party of men in the Pinnace and yawl accompanied by Mr. Banks and Dr. Solander. We landed abreast of the Ship and on the East side of the River just mentioned; but seeing some of the Natives on the other side of the River of whom I was desirous of speaking with, and finding that we could not ford the River, I order'd the yawl in to carry us over, and the pinnace to lay at the Entrance. In the mean time the Indians made off. However we went as far as their Hutts which lay about 2 or 300 Yards from the water side, leaving 4 boys to take care of the Yawl, which we had no sooner left than 4 Men came out of the woods on the other side the River, and would certainly have cut her off had not the People in the Pinnace discover'd them and called to her to drop down the Stream, which they did, being closely persued by the Indians. The coxswain of the Pinnace, who had the charge of the Boats, seeing this, fir'd 2 Musquets over their Heads; the first made them stop and Look round them, but the 2nd they took no notice of; upon which a third was fir'd and kill'd one of them upon the Spot just as he was going to dart his spear at the Boat. At this the other 3 stood motionless for a Minute or two, seemingly quite surprised; wondering, no doubt, what it was that had thus kill'd their Comrade; but as soon as they recovered themselves they made off, dragging the Dead body a little way and then left it. Upon our hearing the report of the Musquets we immediately repair'd to the Boats, and after viewing the Dead body we return'd on board."

Over the following weeks, Cook devoted himself to making a detailed map of the New Zealand coast. Sailing west, Cook hoped to reach Van Diemen's Land, known today as Tasmania, but instead, the winds forced him north, leading him and his men to the southeastern coast of Australia.

Cook

A replica of Cook's ship, *Endeavour*

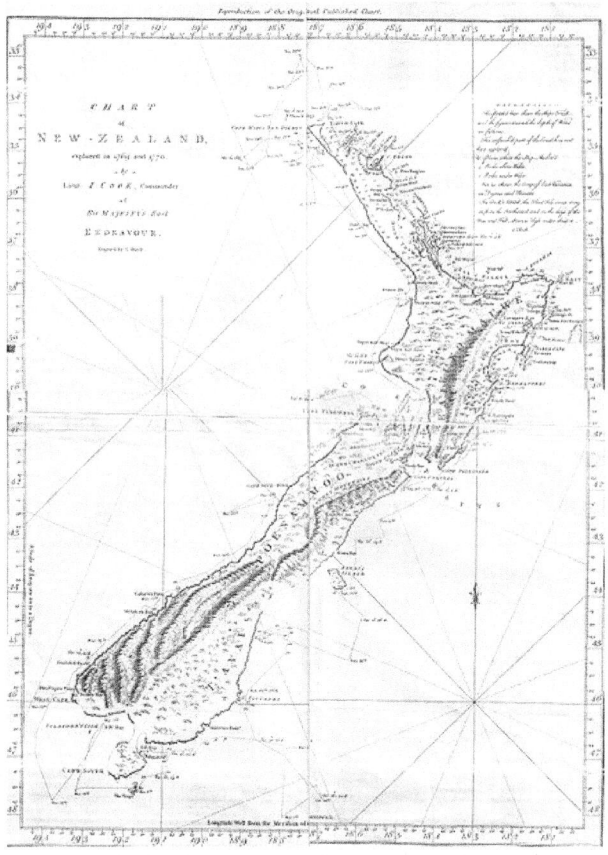

Cook's map of New Zealand's shore

Thus, it was Cook who would Anglicize the name to New Zealand, and on both of his subsequent voyages, Cook returned to New Zealand, but only to cruise the coast and touch lightly on the shore.

Cook's expedition may have been for the purposes of science on the surface, but when he claimed the new territory, the British realized it might serve as a center of future British maritime power and trade in the region. Indeed, as it turned out, that region that would soon be of significant interest to the British because of the American Revolution.

The American colonists, although patriotic and committed, could never have taken on the

British Empire unassisted. A vast anti-British coalition formed in Europe, which provided the political, economic and material bulwark of the Revolution. Russia's Catherine the Great was the prime mover in what came to be known as the League of Armed Neutrality, which facilitated the free flow of money and materiel to North America, provided as aid and assistance by the non-belligerent powers. These, although hardly non-belligerent, included France, which was almost never unwilling to oppose the English, as well as Prussia, the Holy Roman Empire, the Netherlands, Portugal, Spain, and Ottoman Turkey.

After the 1783 Treaty of Paris, the British and the new United States somewhat reconciled, while the French, Dutch, and Spanish continued their bitterly anti-English campaign. In combination, they outstripped British maritime power, and they were in a position to challenge British trade with India and China, the cornerstone of the colossal wealth machine that was British East Indian trade.

At the time, the broad pattern of British trade saw British ships embarking south from England, sailing with the currents across the Atlantic, before striking east via the Cape of Good Hope to India. They would then load up on opium grown under duress by the Indians and ship it to China, where it was sold under duress to the Chinese. For the return journey, tea and various other exotic produce from India were acquired.

Vital to this trade equation was the Cape of Good Hope, a Dutch possession since 1652, and a pivotal strategic maritime position. As far as the British were concerned, the Cape of Good Hope was, at least for the time being, the weak link in the chain. The Dutch were allied with the French, and in addition to the Cape of Good Hope, the Dutch also held the important Ceylonese port of Trincomalee, from which they and their French allies were in a position to threaten British India and British trade interests throughout the region.

If push came to shove and the Cape of Good Hope became unavailable, the British trading fleet would be forced to utilize the east coast of South America, dealing with numerous Spanish and Spanish allied regimes inimical to the British, after which the Cape Horn or Magellan Straits would require negotiation before the long haul across the South Pacific to India. This would certainly not have been ideal.

Then there was the more subtle question of basic raw materials. The Royal Navy, the largest single maritime force in existence, had stripped the British Isles of timber reserves to the extent that a fleet of wooden ships could not be domestically sustained. British timber supplies that supported the local ship-building industries not only came mainly from Russia, but also other Baltic nations. However, in the aftermath of the American Revolution, Russia had become rather estranged and could no longer entirely be trusted. An average Royal Navy or merchant ship of the line utilized more than one mast, which was often several hundred feet tall, and these frequently required repair and replacement. So did the sails and the ships themselves. Denmark and Sweden, alternative sources of timber for the British, were also now of uncertain status, having signed on with the Russian sponsored pro-American League of Armed Neutrality.

It certainly was a hostile world for the British in the late 18th century, even as the British stood to benefit most from international trade. The Royal Navy and the British maritime fleet dominated the major maritime trade routes, but they did so from a position with almost no friends, and ultimately, if Britain could not rely on the cooperation of any other European powers, then the alternative was simply to make do alone. Cook happened to be of the opinion that the only major sources of timber and flax in the Pacific region were to be found in New Zealand and Norfolk Island, located some 1,000 miles northeast of Botany Bay. Nonetheless, it was his opinion that Botany Bay represented the most viable location for a permanent British colony.

Meanwhile, the anti-British alliance continued to ferment in the aftermath of the French Revolution. The French were deeply embittered by their ejection from North America, and for that matter, so were the British, but there was little to be gained by either side crying over spilled milk. However, the French remained deeply interested in India, which was still not comprehensively dominated by the British, and thus still vulnerable to a robust French effort at a takeover. In fact, the French were negotiating a treaty with Ottoman Egypt that would allow French use of Egyptian soil in general communication with her surviving outposts in India. Those outposts were fortified with apparently decommissioned gunships, and a military alliance was formalized with the Dutch for the use of port facilities at the Cape of Good Hope and other Dutch bases in the Pacific.

As a result, in the wake of Cook's voyages, a robust body of commercial explorers, the European whaling fleet, began to probe the New Zealand shoreline for whales and fur seals. It was they who founded the first settlements, and they made substantive contact with the Māoris. Contact in this case was more sustained and engaged, so trade took place, and goods and commodities changed hands. For the first time, the Māoris were introduced to metal, and the potential and value of trade was realized.

More importantly, the value of guns was realized, and for a martial people, this certainly must have been a seminal moment. The potential of this technology was immediately apprehended, and almost instantly the tempo and intensity of internal warfare increased. This is an era of the history of New Zealand known as the "Musket Wars," and alternatively, the "Māori Holocaust," which is probably more accurate.

The Māori began acquiring muskets in trade with itinerate whalers and seal hunters almost at the moment that the two cultures met. Later, at the turn of the 19th century, flax and timber traders from Port Jackson and Sydney began shipping in large quantities. The first internal conflicts that came about as a consequence of this were recorded in and around the northern tip of North Island, beginning in about 1807 or 1808. This was the "Battle of Moremonui," fought between the *Ngāpuhi* and *Ngāti Whātua* in Northland, not far from present-day Dargaville.

What is interesting about this brief conflict is that one side, the Ngāpuhi, had muskets, but they had not mastered their use sufficiently to overwhelm an opposing force of similar size armed with traditional weapons, and they were ultimately defeated. The early firearms that found their way into Māori hands were of very dubious quality, and generally in poor condition. Historians have tended, therefore, to describe the part played by early musketry in Māori warfare as "shock and awe." In much the same way Abel Tasman's release of a canister of shot sent the Māori scampering, so the same was true for any group encountering guns for the first time.

Before long, members of the *Ngāti Korokoro hapū* clan of Ngāpuhi were delivered a second major defeat when a raid on the neighboring *Kai Tutae* iwi was defeated despite the fact they outnumbered the enemy 10-1. This was simply because the *Kai Tutae* had equipped themselves with more and better muskets. This became the pattern, and a kind of arms race soon began. The various iwi began amassing weapons and launched heavier and more aggressive raids on one another, developing a slave economy that produced both food and flax for export, in exchange, of course, for more guns.

A secondary trade in smoked heads, or *mokomokai*, also developed as something of a byproduct of war. These satisfied the macabre curiosity of visiting Europeans, who accepted them as trade items. Before long, no governor's lodge, civil servant's office, or club bar was complete without one.[4] In part because of their value, raids were being carried out purely to acquire more heads, which were hastily preserved and sold. Prisoners of war and slaves were killed, with their heads randomly tattooed and preserved for sale. In 1931, the Governor of New South Wales, General Sir Ralph Darling, was driven by the slaughter to issue a ban on any further trade in smoked heads from New Zealand.

In 1821, Hongi Hika, *rangatira* (chief) and war leader of the Ngāpuhi, traveled to England

---

[4] *Mokomokai*, or smoked heads, was a traditional Māori practice of preserving the heads of fallen enemies, and other deceased. This was originally ceremonial, but with the rush to acquire guns, they were freely traded.

with the Anglican missionary Thomas Kendall, and on his return, called in at Sydney and traded the many gifts he had received for between 300 and 500 muskets. He then used the guns to mount raids across a much greater area.

The effects of all of this on the wider Māori society were obviously devastating. Sometime in 1835, warriors of the *Ngāti Mutunga, Ngāti Tama* and *Ngāti Toa* hijacked a British ship to carry them to the Chatham Islands, and there they fell upon and slaughtered about 10% of the Moriori, enslaving the survivors, but then descending inevitably into war between themselves.

Tactically, muskets in the hands of a detachment of marauding Māori warriors had limited offensive value, usually because they were inaccurate and the musketeers themselves had no training. Their main use, therefore, was in creating a situation of confusion to allow more traditional infantrymen to rush the enemy and defeat them with traditional weapons.

However, as proficiency and technology improved, muskets began to be employed directly in battle. Double-barrels were preferred, and occasional modifications were made. Often in battle, women were used to rapidly reload the weapons.

Until 1841, New Zealand, as a British dependency, was administered as part of New South Wales, and for the most part, wars and conflicts between different groups of Māori in New Zealand did not impact the very thin veneer of white settlement in just a handful of places. However, at the moment that an armed and restive Māori population began to potentially threaten European interests, the authorities acted, and legal limitations on the sale of firearms to the Māori began to creep into the territorial statute. The first of these was the "Arms, Gunpowder and other Warlike Stores Act of 1845," followed in 1846 by the "Arms Ordinance," and later still the "Gunpowder Ordinance Act 1847."

These limitations, the exhaustion of the warring groups, and a general spread of the rule of law put an end to much of the fighting, and while there was no truly official end for the Musket Wars, the fighting was largely over by 1842. During the thousands of individual skirmishes and battles, somewhere between 20,000-40,000 Māori lost their lives.[5] The end of the Musket Wars also marked the point that white interests and priorities began to predominate.

Missionaries and Whalers

"[T]he signal for the dawn of civilization, liberty, and religion in that dark and benighted land."
- Reverend Samuel Marsden, 1814

As was the case in almost every British overseas territory, the vanguard of settlement and pacification was the Christian missionary movement. The nationality and denomination of early hunters and traders invariably tended to influence the language and denomination of the first

---
[5] The Musket Wars were also known as the "Potato Wars." The name "Potato Wars" refers to the introduction of potatoes at about the same time as muskets which allowed for enough of a food surplus for iwi to concentrate on warfare with less effort needed to provide food.

missionaries, but it was always the missionaries who tested the waters and prepared the ground for future arrivals, founding the basic infrastructure of settlements and preparing the way for the establishment of formal dependencies.

They also, in many respects, provided a cultural bridge between the old and the new. The natives of any such territory, in this case the Māori, were introduced to the religion, language, and culture of the newcomers long before the pressures and realities of a colonial annexation were felt. The price of this was conversion, and the systematic destruction of traditional lifestyles, practices, and values. The spread of Christianity by this means depended often on the state of mind of those being converted. In Africa, for example, the absolute destruction by slavery and white rule of traditional societies created a vacuum, and Christianity filled that vacuum. Conversely, in places like India and New Zealand, indigenous belief structures remained strong, and Christianity did not make quite the same robust headway.

In the late 1700s, Christianity was superficially introduced to New Zealand by early traders and settlers, but this was simply by osmosis, not by conversion. It was not until 1814, when the first Protestant missionaries, members of the British Anglican Church Missionary Society, arrived on the shores of the two islands that formal Christianity appeared. The enterprise was delayed a little by an event known as the Boyd Massacre, which took place in 1809. The *Boyd* was a convict ship that sailed from Port Jackson in October 1809 to collect a cargo of timber from Whangaroa Harbor on the northern tip of North Island. For reasons that have never been clear, the crew of the ship, up to 70 men, were overrun, killed and eaten by local Māori, one of the largest massacres of Europeans in the early history of New Zealand, and one of the bloodiest episodes of cannibalism on record.

An 1889 painting of the *Boyd* blowing up

Catholicism arrived on the islands somewhat later. It was first introduced by Irish and French seamen and traders, and some early missionary work was attempted, but the first organized Catholic mission did not appear in New Zealand until formally introduced by the French in the 1830s.

Missionaries usually followed the first trading contacts, and in this case whaling represented the first and most obvious economic attraction of New Zealand's coastal waters. The harvesting of whales was an enormous industry at the time, competing only with the harvesting of ivory in Africa as a wildlife commodity that fed the Industrial Revolution. Whale blubber was used in illumination, various types of fuel, in oils for industry and armaments, and in numerous food products. Bones were used for fashion, instrumentation and construction. As early as 1791, the first whaler, the *William and Anne*, under Captain Ebner Bunker, appeared in New Zealand waters. The *William and Anne* set sail from England in March 1791 as part of the "Third Fleet," transporting goods and convicts to the penal colony of New South Wales on Australia.[6] The hunt for sperm whales in the South Pacific was a brief side venture, and there is no record that any whales were actually caught.

Nonetheless, by the turn of the century, whaling had become a thriving industry along the coast of New Zealand, with British, American, and French fleets regularly visiting the islands. This

---

[6] The First, Second and Third Fleets were waves of convict transportation dispatched from England to New South Wales between 1787 and 1792.

had the effect of establishing a small fraternity of Māori crewmen who joined the ships when they arrived onshore, and others who became permanently engaged as maritime merchant crew. By the mid-19th century, more than 100 shore bases had been established, although by then whale populations had begun to decline, and diminished returns saw many of these settlements abandoned soon afterwards.

In the meanwhile, the *Britannia*, another ship of the Third Fleet disembarked 188 convicts in Port Jackson and intended to divert to China en-route back to England in order to collect a cargo of tea. Although nominally interested in whale blubber, a more lucrative cargo in the form of fur seal pelts presented itself as the *Britannia* cruised the west coast of South Island. Men were dropped off, and in 10 months they were able to amass a haul of 4,500 skins. Fur seals were also to be found in significant numbers in the Bass Strait, along the Great Australian Bight and on the south shore of Tasmania. It was not really until these sources had begun to diminish that the industry picked up in New Zealand, but by 1830, seals had been hunted almost to extinction along the entire coast of New Zealand, and hunting was eventually banned in 1926.

Following these early whalers, the first Church Missionary Society station was established by Reverend Samuel Marsden in the Bay of Islands on the northern peninsular of North Island. This became the site of the first identifiable European town in New Zealand, then known by the Māori name as *Kororāreka*, but now known as Old Russell. The mission and the settlement were established at the confluence of old trade contacts between various commercial seamen and the local Māori. The Māori produced potatoes and pork, and in exchange for these, firearms and other sundry trade goods were bartered.

Marsden

The missionaries, however, encountered a violent and dissolute settlement, made worse by the effects of the gun trade in the hinterland and the general state of insecurity of the surrounding countryside. Missionary relations with the administration in Sydney were uncooperative, and certainly there was little early interest among the Māori in any moral currency the missionaries might have to trade - the Māori wanted the salvation of guns, not Christ.

Nonetheless, by 1840, mission stations had been established at Kaitaia, Thames, Whangaroa, Waikato, Mamamata, Rotorua, Tauranga, Manukau and Poverty Bay. Schools and hospitals were built, and the first efforts to educate the Māori youth began. By 1840, over 20 stations had been founded, most of which were on North Island, and all of which, to a greater or lesser extent, later evolved into towns and cities.

In many respects, the missionaries competed with the traders and hunters for the hearts and minds of the Māori population. As an alternative to guns and alcohol, the missionaries offered conversion, the development of a written form of their language, basic education, health and sanitation, and improved farming methods. As already noted, the missionaries offered a sympathetic cultural bridge and a soft landing as European influence penetrated ever deeper into the Māori cultural hinterland.

Indeed, from this initial missionary experience, a great many reflections and memoirs found their way into print, and from these sources, it is clear that the mission establishment was very hostile to the forces of trade and colonization. Trade and colonization brought out the worst in both sides. White traders and settlers tended to introduce disease, alcohol, and firearms, which attracted the most violent and corrupted elements of Māori society. Sexually transmitted diseases were rife in these communities, and offspring born as a result of contact between the two sides found themselves shunned by both cultures.

The irony perhaps is that the missionaries introduced their own corrosive ideologies and practices, and they were no less disdainful of ancient traditional practice than any other. They were jealous of the moral turf, and they did not encourage unaffiliated white settlement. Nonetheless, as the forces of trade and colonization grew more organized and ubiquitous, the missionaries bent to the inevitable, and in the end they were instrumental in persuading the Māori leadership to accept the terms of the iconic "Treaty of Waitangi."

The Founding of a Colony

"Governor, you should stay with us and be like a father. If you go away then the French or the rum sellers will take us Māori people over." - Chief Hōne Heke

The British colony of New South Wales was founded in 1788 upon the arrival of what is known as the First Fleet. This was the first formal expedition to establish a penal colony on the east coast of Australia, then known as New Holland. At the same time, the commission of the first Governor of New Zealand, Captain Arthur Phillip, included a broad remit on administrative responsibility for an area vaguely defined as encompassing "all the islands adjacent in the Pacific Ocean within the latitudes of 10°37'S and 43°39'S." This overlapped most of New Zealand, with the exception of the southern half of South Island.

Phillip

In 1825, Van Diemen's Land, the future Tasmania, was detached to form a separate colony under domestic administration, and as part of the reshuffle, the boundary of New South Wales was extended to include the islands adjacent in the Pacific Ocean, with a southern boundary of 39°12'S. This diminished the area of New Zealand under the control of New South Wales to only the northern half of North Island.

None of this was of much consequence on the ground since the extension of administrative control from Sydney was in any case academic. Interest at the time was focused on the mainland of *Terra Australis*, and developing the various settlements that sprung up on sundry parts of the Australian coast. There were, however, pockets of permanent white settlement taking place in a disordered and irregular manner, and there were, of course, the first shoots of missionary settlement. New Zealand became a popular destination for British fugitives from justice since no formal law existed on the islands, and so the first formal inclusion of New Zealand under a British administrative remit was legal.

Various legal statutes originating in the British Imperial Parliament brought the territory of New Zealand effectively under British law. The "Murders Abroad Act of 1817" was one of these, and although it was not specifically aimed at New Zealand, it allowed the authorities in New South Wales to legally pursue fugitives in New Zealand, and to ensure that no corner of the region could be claimed as a safe haven from British justice. Typically it fell on the judiciary of New South Wales to enforce any application of this Act in New Zealand.

The Murders Abroad Act was followed up in 1823 by a much more muscular and specific article of legislation, the "New South Wales Act of 1823," which placed under the jurisdiction of the Supreme Court of New South Wales all of the New Zealand territories.

The first official British presence in New Zealand was the appointment of a Resident named James Busby, a Scottish born immigrant to Australia who took up his appointment in the Bay of Islands settlement in March 1833. An official Resident was a diplomatic position with no specific powers other than to observe and report, but some authority did come with this appointment, even if it was a long way short of a consular appointment or a governorship. This appointment came about largely as a consequence of ongoing complaints by members of the Church Missionary Society of rampant lawlessness in the various settlements of North Island.

James Busby was an interesting character, and his influence on the early constitutional development of New Zealand was quite profound. He was born in Scotland, the son of the influencial engineer John Busby, and arrived in New South Wales with his family in 1824 at the age of 22. He was a viticulturalist by inclination and training, and his were the first vines planted in Australia. He was 30 when he arrived in New Zealand, and he was immediately captivated by what he saw. He built a home at Waitangi, and there he planted a vineyard from where the first wine in the colony was produced, reaching production even before the vines planted earlier in New South Wales.

Busby

Besides founding the wine industries of both colonies, Busby's official duties were to protect British commerce, to arbitrate in any disputes, and to act as mediator between unruly settlers and the sometimes no less unruly Māori. This was necessary because the Māori of New Zealand were by no means the fractured and inoffensive Aborigines of Australia, who withered away at almost their first contact with whites. Contacts between the whites and the Māori in New Zealand had the potential to be very violent indeed, and the standard of lawlessness in New Zealand made New South Wales, notwithstanding its predominantly convict population, seem like a playground by comparison.

In 1835, a rumor reached Busby that a French nobleman, the Baron Charles Philippe Hippolyte de Thierry, was intending to declare French sovereignty over the islands of New Zealand, which, under international convention, if not law, would certainly have carried some weight.[7] As a Resident, Busby represented the British Crown on the islands only, and as yet no formal act of annexation had been taken. Wasting no time, Busby, who had established a good network of diplomatic relations with the various Māori iwi, drafted a declaration of independence, which was signed at a meeting of 35 chiefs controlling most of North Island. What was created was ostensibly "The United Tribes of New Zealand."

This was an audacious move, and it might, under different circumstances, have worked. No French baron in the end had any real chance of securing control of the islands, but the possibility of an independent confederation of Māori tribes was intriguing, and bearing in mind the advanced state of development of the Māori, it was not utterly inconceivable. A similar attempt by the Australian Aborigines would have reaped such howls of derision that no one would have ever thought to try it. Māori emissaries and diplomats, on the other hand, had already visited New South Wales and England, and they were engaged on a diplomatic level with the ruling establishments of both. The Māori were engaged in international trade, some owned ships, some were educated, and in the absence of any other form of government on the island, the idea of a Māori government on some level was not treated as being utterly outlandish.

It is probably worth noting that the British Imperial Government, then at a fairly formative phase, would in quite a number of cases overlay British imperial superintendence over a native government as a means of administering a territory or dependency indirectly. The best example of this might be the "Dual Mandate" concept of Lord Frederick Lugard, in the British protectorate of Northern Nigeria. There, the various sultanates and emirates of the region remained intact, ruling in a manner disturbed only by very loosely applied British supervision. The advantage of this to the British was that their government came at a cheap price, and to the traditional leadership, access to modern systems of administration and government, compatible with any other, came without any radical modification to the traditional system.

---

[7] Baron de Thierry was in fact intending to establish a settlement, not a colony, which is somewhat different, but Busby made use of the rumor nonetheless.

Busby's declaration of independence entered a gray legal area, and in most instances, it was regarded as a curiosity without any particular force. It was rewarded with recognition from nowhere, and if it did have legal merit, that fell away with the later signing of the "Treaty of Waitangi." The signing of this treaty was one of the seminal milestones of New Zealand constitutional history, and it is a fascinating example of not only the inexorability, but also the adaptability of British imperial expansion.

From 1835-1840, the Colonial Office dithered over precisely what to do with New Zealand. In the spring of 1836, the Governor of New South Wales, Sir Richard Bourke, dispatched a naval expedition under the command of Captain William Hobson to visit New Zealand in order to investigate firsthand the situation in the territory. Hobson's recommendation was simply that British sovereignty be declared over limited areas of British and European settlement, with a view then to an incremental increase in claims over the entire territory. This report was forwarded to the Colonial Office for consideration, and in the spring of 1838, a House of Lords Select Committee met to consider the "State of the Islands of New Zealand." Submissions were made by various bodies, including private, public, commercial, and religious interests. This resulted in Letters Patent issued to expand the territorial scope of New South Wales to include both the North and South Islands of New Zealand in their entirety. The Governor of New South Wales, then Sir George Gipps, was formally given the additional responsibility of Governor of New Zealand.

Hobson

This, then, was the first clear statement of intent on the part of the British Imperial Government that it intended to make a formal claim over New Zealand. Prior to this, Hobson's suggestion of limited British sovereignty was weighed up, and although very nearly reaching a consensus, did not quite. The idea as it was discussed in Whitehall was simply for a "Māori State," perhaps even a republic, within which British settlers were guaranteed certain rights of land and representation. In the end, a full settler state was agreed to, and in practical terms, the declaration of independence was immediately rendered moot.

Hobson was then appointed British Consul to New Zealand, and to him fell the task of establishing the constitutional framework of a new colony, and also of negotiating the surrender of Māori sovereignty to the British Crown. Under instructions from the Home Secretary, the Marquis of Normanby, Hobson was to "seek a cession of sovereignty, to assume complete control over land matters, and to establish a form of civil government." No draft treaty was given to him to work with, however, so he was left largely to his own resources to create the necessary instruments.

The official British position, as these steps were being taken, was ostensibly to protect Māori interests. This idea lay very much at the fore of the imperial establishment at the time. The traditional view of the British Empire is that it was a rapacious, exploitative and violent institution that left the destroyed remains of native society in its wake. This was more the attitude of the settler communities themselves, and quite often the Imperial Government was at odds with overseas colonies over precisely this question. In 1837, for example, a British Parliamentary Select Committee sat to examine the state and condition of all aboriginal subjects of Her Majesty. The Committee met "to consider what measures ought to be adopted with regards to the native inhabitants of the countries where British settlements are made, and to the neighboring tribes, in order to secure to them the due observance of justice, and the protection of their rights; to promote the spread of civilization among them, and to lead them to the peaceful and voluntary reception of the Christian religion."

This was something of a clarion call to missionaries and administrators across the British Empire to pay greater heed to the effects that European settlements were having on the native races of the world. This concern was expressed largely for the natives of North America, the Hottentot of the Cape, and the Aborigines of Australia. The Māori were not held to be in quite the same class as these, and they were not regarded as imperiled in any way, but nonetheless, it was a sensitive issue, and the Imperial Government felt the need to tread warily.

On January 29, 1840 William Hobson arrived in the Bay of Islands, with a ship of the recently chartered New Zealand Company, the *Cuba*, arriving not far behind. This ship carried Company members commissioned to conduct a survey on the feasibility of organized settlement, and to break ground prior to the arrival of shiploads of assisted immigrants. Already anchored in the harbor was the *Aurora*, carrying the first of these Company settlers. The New Zealand Company was anxious to get all of this done and to take up land before British annexation and the complications that would follow.

The next day was a Thursday, and Hobson wasted no time in calling a general meeting at Christs Church at Kororāreka. By presenting the Letters Patent of 1839, he announced the establishment of British sovereignty, confirmed his own appointment and let it be known that a process of establishing the constitutional basis of the new colony would commence immediately.

The basis of any style of colony could only be consequent to some sort of agreement by treaty with the various Māori iwi. This was clearly understood by all parties, and it cannot therefore be said that the Māori were duped into anything or negotiated with in bad faith. In general, the Māori were respectful of the British at that time. Many Māori served as crewmembers on British ships and thus traveled, with quite a number visiting England. As a result, they had a much clearer sense of the world than many other native peoples at that time. The British were a great maritime and trading nation, and the benefits and ramifications of a grand alliance with them were reasonably understood.

The treaty that followed was carefully drafted and amended by Hobson himself, assisted by Busby as official Resident and Hobson's private secretary James Freeman. None of these men were lawyers, however, so the basic structure of the treaty was borrowed from the text of various preexisting British treaties. It was ready for translation in just four days. From there it was handed over to the missionary Henry Williams, who, along with his son, was fluent in *Te Reo*, the lingua franca of the Māori. It was they who constructed the Māori version of the document. This was done overnight, and on February 5, 1840 it was ready for circulation among the various Māori chiefs.

Williams

In a single sentence of 216 words, Hobson introduced himself as a constituted functionary of Her Majesty Victoria, with powers to establish government, and to control and manage European settlement, both current and pending, and empowered moreover to treat with the Māori. Thereafter, as contained in three articles, all sovereignty was to be ceded to the British Crown, the Māori were guaranteed continued, undisturbed access to their lands and resources, the Crown reserved first right of preemption for any land alienated, and the Māori were guaranteed of all the rights and privileges owed to any other British subjects.

The translation of this document was inevitably imperfect, and in the years since, it has been examined minutely for any evidence of deliberate duplicity, but the findings in general have tended to suggest not. The English and Māori versions of the treaty document are substantially the same, except for one or two subtle differences that might bear accusations of intentional ambiguity. In fact, the difficulty that Henry Williams encountered was in the absence of appropriate Māori language to cover some of the concepts imparted. For example, in Article One, the English version stated that the chiefs were obliged to cede all rights and powers of sovereignty to the Crown, while in the Maori version, the implication is quite different. Here it states that Māori chiefs relinquish all "government" to the Crown, which, of course, implies

Crown responsibility for administration and not full and sovereign overlordship. No direct translation for "sovereignty" exists in Māori, simply because the Māori functioned on the level of individual tribes without any paramount ruler. In a second point, the jumbled and rather chaotic interpretation seems not to have conveyed clearly the concept of "preemption," and the question of land and land purchase as a whole.[8]

Nonetheless, it was this document that was presented to an assembly of northern chiefs inside an expansive marquee erected on the grounds of Busby's home in Waitangi. The document was read aloud, first in English by Hobson, and then in *Te Reo* by Henry Williams. Thereafter, for some five hours, the contents of the draft treaty were debated by the Māori chiefs, and most accounts of the episode tend to portray it as a fractious and angry interlude, with subtle divisions that were not easy for the whites to interpret. There was, for example, division between converted Catholic and Anglican members of the Māori leadership, and this was in part because the small Catholic mission fraternity, mainly French, but also Irish, had been at work urging the chiefs not to trust the British authorities. There was a general resistance to the notion of a "Governor," and the loss of land, and in some instances it was demanded that land already purchased or occupied be returned. That said, the arguments seemed to be formulaic and rather spurious in character, for when the time came to ratify the treaty, 45 chiefs of North Island, representing the majority, presented themselves to sign. In fact, they arrived a day early, on February 6, which forced Hobson to improvise a ceremony.

In the end, it would seem that a rather sophisticated interpretation of the situation convinced the chiefs that the likely benefits of British sovereignty and protection would outweigh the disadvantages. It is also true that those gathering to debate the matter understood quite clearly the international dynamic now at play. If the British were denied constitutional sovereignty by treaty, then they would achieve it in some other way, probably by conquest, and the terms might then not be so generous. Moreover, there were always the French, occupying Polynesian islands where and when they could. Given a chance, they would certainly make a play for New Zealand, and in the grand scheme of things, the British were preferred.

Thus, on February 6, 1840, the "Treaty of Waitaki" was signed, and Busby's home thus acquired the name "Treaty House." Further signatures were later added, and on May 21, 1840, sovereignty was declared over North Island on the basis of the Waitaki Treaty, and over South Island by virtue of prior discovery by Captain James Cook in 1769.

For the time being, however, the colony of New Zealand remained subject to the administrative control of New South Wales, and Hobson was appointed Lieutenant Governor answerable to the Governor of New South Wales. The "Charter for Erecting the Colony of New Zealand" was issued by Letters Patent on November 16, 1840 which stated in its preamble that New Zealand

---

[8] "Preemption" is described by the Oxford Dictionary as the purchase of goods or shares by one person or party before the opportunity is offered to others.

would gain the status of the crown Colony separate from New South Wales on July 1, 1841.

Immigration and Settlement

"[F]raudulent debtors…have escaped from their creditors in Sydney or Hobart Town, and needy adventurers from the two colonies, almost unequally unprincipled." – John Dunmore Lang

For a long time, New Zealand was regarded purely as a commercial resource of New South Whales, and most of the early economic activity that increasingly introduced permanent settlement to the islands originated in New South Wales. It was merchants from Sydney, and later Hobart who pioneered the flax, timber, fur seal and whaling industries, and Sydney was the base from which the first Christian missions found their way to New Zealand.

The first recorded permanent settlement was in Dusky Sound, in 1792, located amongst the beautiful fjords of South Island. This was an insubstantial settlement that did not survive long. The 1825 settlement of Codfish Island, to the northwest of Stewart Island, in the extreme south of South Island, lasted a little longer, but it was soon shifted across the strait to Stewart Island, and then on to the mainland. These were all sealing and whaling depots, without any particular pretense at permanence. Those that began the exploit the timber reserves of the islands, concentrated mostly along the windward slopes of South Island, and in pockets of North Island, became the first of what might be regarded as permanent settlements. The timber of the region offered up a very necessary resource in the age of wooden ships, and once discovered, an organized timber industry, centered in Sydney, quickly kicked into gear. By 1816, the first cargoes of timber sawn and processed in New Zealand by permanently settled sawyers began to arrive in Sydney.

A census conducted in 1836 revealed that fully a third of all permanently settled European males in New Zealand were engaged in timber processing and export. Shore-based whaling operations were established soon afterwards, mainly along the east coast from Foveaux Strait, at the southern tip of South Island, to East Cape, the eastern-most point of North Island. By 1830, or thereabouts, some fifteen Sydney based firms and companies were managing twenty-two separate whaling settlements within this region. Some of these were quite substantial, for example in the Bay of Plenty, but others were sparsely populated and transitory.

The demographic was mixed, with many Māori engaged, and a steady interaction between settler men and Māori women occurred, with the inevitable result. Convicts, army and navy deserters and many others made up a population mainly of men, somewhat predisposed to violence and crime, and inclined towards dissolute habits. Fugitive convicts from the penal settlements of Australia were recorded in the Bay of Islands as early 1815, a fact observed by Charles Darwin when he visited the site in 1835. In 1837, the *Sydney Herald* estimated a population of between 200 and 300 escaped convicts in New Zealand, mainly in the Bay of Islands.

Among these were a group known as the *Pākehā Māori*, from the word Pākehā, the general Māori term for a white or European person. The Pākehā Māori were simply white men forced for one reason or another to take refuge in Māori communities, beyond the reach of British justice. One can assume, therefore, that most of these were escaped convicts and general fugitives although there certainly were those who entered that life as a matter of preference and were content within it. In rare instances, whites were held by the Māori as slaves although this certainly was rare. The number of Pākehā Māori in 1830 was about fifty, and a decade later about 150. Most were either English or Irish, and a majority appear to have rejoined white society more or less as British sovereignty was declared.

The missionaries, of course, represented another demographic, and as we have already heard, the first permanent missionaries arrived as part of the Church Missionary Society initiative, led by the Reverend Samuel Marsden in 1814. Many of the dispersed mission stations that were seeded from the initial settlement in the Bay of Islands became the basis of later towns and cities. On the eve of British sovereignty in 1840, Church and Wesleyan Missionary Society missionaries, and their families, numbered 206.

Then there were the free settlers, a sporadic addition to the commercial and missionary populations, and again mostly drifting across from New South Wales and other Australian settlements. The pace of free immigration began to quicken as the date of British annexation neared. This was partly because the establishment of a British colony required not only the recruitment of administrative personnel to take up various functions of government and the judiciary, but also because the development of a capital and the various construction and building projects associated with this further demanded the importation of skilled labor, many of whom brought their families. It is also true that land occupied prior to annexation was generally regarded as a *fait accompli*, so there were many attempting to gain land before a British administration could be introduced on the islands.

All of this also happened to coincide with the drought in New South Wales, the steady increase in the price of land and diminishing scope for settlement. The Swan River Settlement in Western Australia, a bold experiment in systematic settlement, had fared poorly, and a number of disappointed colonists from this region eventually made their way to New Zealand. New Zealand offered a new land with fresh opportunities, and as the century progressed, many people were alerted to this.

The first capital of New Zealand was Old Russell, now the small settlement of Okiato, some five miles south of present-day Ruddell in the Bay of Islands. In 1841, after the signing of the Treaty of Waitaki, the seat of government was shifted to the settlement of Auckland, named after the then Viceroy of India, the Earl of Auckland. The land was gifted to the government by the Ngāti Whātua, a local iwi as a gesture of goodwill.

Settlements were already beginning to form at Wellington and Nelson, in the Cook Strait, and recognizing in due course that the former offered a more central location for the administration of both islands, the territorial capital was moved to Wellington in 1865.

The attributes of New Zealand as a destination for British emigration were by the first decades of the 19th century well appreciated. The islands, in particular North Island, enjoyed a temperate climate suitable for European settlement, and fertile soils that were well drained and watered. Several attempts were made to organize systematic settlement, and although ultimately unsuccessful, they did succeed in introducing small numbers of fresh arrivals.

The first attempt was made in 1825, with the founding of the New Zealand Association, established in England to facilitate immigration to New Zealand, and to seek entry on a large scale into the flax, timber, whaling and fur industries. Somewhat as a by-product of this, organized immigration was also part of the New Zealand Association's plan. The New Zealand Association was superseded in 1825 by the New Zealand Company, which was not awarded its Royal Charter until 1841. At its founding, the Company unsuccessfully petitioned the British Imperial Government for a thirty-one-year period of exclusive trade, along with the right to settle the territory, and establish an army. Royal chartered companies were typically granted rights along these lines, examples of which, of course, are the Hudson Bay Company and the British East India Company. Trade in New Zealand was already dispersed quite widely by then, and a monopoly simply would not have been possible. The use of private armies, along the lines of the Indian Army, was not an attractive idea in New Zealand, because war would have been inevitable, and the British Imperial Government would have been required inevitably to intercede.

Nevertheless, the following year, the New Zealand Company dispatched two ships, the *Lambton* and the *Isabella*, under the command of Captain James Herd, to examine trade prospects and identify potential settlements. Sometime in September or October of 1826, the two ships dropped anchor in the Cook Straits, in present day Wellington Harbor which was very quickly established as a suitable site for permanent settlement. A million acres of land was supposedly purchased from the Māori although no documentation to this effect is in existence, and certainly nothing came of it.

The next venture of this kind, also underwritten by the New Zealand Company, was the voyage of the ship *Tory*, which anchored in Port Nicholson in August 1939, also with a view to identifying and purchasing likely sites for organized settlement. The first immigrant ship, the *Aurora*, of which we have already heard, arrived in Wellington Harbor in January 1840. Named after the Duke of Wellington, the proposed settlement was part of the New Zealand Companies model of organized colonization. This model, incidentally, was conceived and developed by Edward Gibbon Wakefield, a colorful character who was involved in quite a number of similar schemes in Australia and Canada before his engagement with the New Zealand Company.

Again, part of the haste in reforming the New Zealand Company, and then attempting to establish settlements in New Zealand had to do with pending British Imperial plans to establish a crown colony in New Zealand, after which the freebooting acquisition of land would be impossible. Wakefield, by then a forty-three-year-old adventurer with a highly checkered past, was invited to join the Company as a director. His philosophy was simply, *"Possess yourself of the Soil and you are Secure."*[9]

The Wakefield Plan simply envisaged packages of land comprising a "town acre," accompanied by 100 country acres, and 1,100 such one-acre town sections were planned for Port Nicholson. This, then, became the basis for the settlement and establishment of Wellington, followed in 1840 by Wanganui, in 1841 by New Plymouth and Nelson in 1842. Some efforts were also made to survey possible sites on South Island. The economic basis of all of this was the idea that large tracts of land would be acquired by purchase from the Māori which would then be parceled up for sale to prospective immigrants.

The Company quickly ran into financial difficulties. For the plan to succeed, higher land prices would need to attract reasonably wealthy colonists whose land purchases would then fund the free immigration of those needed to work the land and build the settlements. In the end there always seemed to be more impoverished immigrants subscribing for assisted passage than those willing to pay for it. In 1844, the Company ceased active trading, and surrendered its charter in 1850. The Company's debts were initially assumed by the British Government, but these were passed on to the New Zealand government in 1854.

Nonetheless, a momentum had begun, and over the next few years, over 8,600 colonists arrived in New Zealand in some 57 ships. By 1859, non-Māori represented the majority population of New Zealand, with over 100,000 English, Scottish and Welsh immigrants permanently settled in New Zealand.

The Exploration of New Zealand's Interior

The exploration of Australia ran along two parallel lines, with the practical exploration of men incrementally spreading settlements outward and the more expedition-orientated exploration exemplified by the likes of the Burke-Wills Expedition. New Zealand presented a very different prospect to early explorers than Australia, mostly because the land is green and pleasant. Another fact was the relationship between the Māori and white man, which was more equal than that between the white man and Aborigines, perhaps more akin to the contact of the white man and natives in North America. Māori guides were easy to find, their knowledge was comprehensive, and they understood trade and remuneration.

Captain Cook himself had returned with what might be regarded as complete reports on the nature of the New Zealand coastline, having completed a circumnavigation of North Island in

---

[9] Edward Gibbon Wakefield was perhaps most widely known for an episode known as the "Shrigley Abduction," during which he abducted a fifteen-year-old heiress and forced her to marry him, for which he and his brother received a three-year prison sentence.

February 1770 and establishing that it was indeed an island. With that, his expedition made clear New Zealand was not part of *Terra Australis*. He had also observed the Banks Peninsula, part of modern Christchurch, which he assumed was an island, and thus it was named Banks Island incidentally after the great naturalist of the age, Sir Joseph Banks.

Cook also observed, at least in passing, the accommodating nature of the landscape, the agreeable climate, and the vigorous nature of the indigenous people. From that point onwards, the mapping of the coast of New Zealand was undertaken almost entirely by visiting sealers, whalers and merchant vessels, plying their various trades and plotting the intricacies of the coastline. For example, in 1804, American sealer Owen Smith discovered Foveaux Strait, which divides Stewart Island from the mainland, and disproved Cook's theory that the Island was part of the mainland. Likewise, in 1809, the English survey ship *Pegasus*, under Captain Samuel Chase, established that Banks Island was, in fact, Banks Peninsular, and the bay thus mapped was for a while known as "Cook's Mistake" before it was later changed to "Pegasus Bay."

The exploration of the interior of the two islands would be a more complex and long-term undertaking, but it would also be a gentler experience than European exploration and colonization taking place across other regions of the world. From the moment Europeans saw the the North and South Islands rising out of the Pacific, the assumption was that New Zealand would be a venue for European emigration. It was perceived as largely empty, and its fertile aspects and pleasant climate were immediate attractions. Settlers began to accumulate at the coast long before any kind of formal administration or control, and certainly before any efforts to explore the interior.

The early explorers were simply ordinary people, driven by curiosity looking around. This was very different from the professional exploration of Africa, for example, which was driven by geographic conundrums such as the Source of the Nile, and Australia, where the question was one of survival against the elements. In New Zealand, the exploration drive was fundamental to settlement, identifying resources, discovering areas of arable land, and finding practical routes to get to them.

Familiar names were given to places and features that offered a comforting familiarity to those who might want to move to New Zealand. To the many reading the promotional literature of the New Zealand Company as it sought to promote the territory as a home for impoverished and wealthy Englishmen alike, names like Wellington, Nelson, Invercargill, Auckland and Christchurch all seemed very welcoming. Artists rendered landscapes for reproduction that were wild enough to be exotic, but green enough to be a fair substitute for England.

The first to arrive with a view to permanent settlement were the missionaries, and interestingly, they did their best to discourage commercial activities and other settlement activities on either of the islands, believing that their presence alone was beneficial to the natives while all others were corrosive. Ironically, it was in the search for fresh missionary fields that the missionaries contributed most to an early understanding of the territory. Samuel Marsden, who was the first missionary to make landfall in New Zealand, arrived in the Bay of Islands in December 1814. The expedition set off from Port Jackson in New South Wales as an outreach of the Australian Anglican missionary movement, and it set off with the support and endorsement of the New South Wales Governor. Marsden purchased land at Rangihoua, and there the first formal mission in New Zealand was established.

Thereafter, Marsden himself, when visiting New Zealand, tramped for hundreds of miles across North Island, visiting remote communities, preaching the gospel, and familiarizing himself with the population. In general, he was kindly received, and in his journals and reports, a picture of the interior geography of North Island began to emerge.

In his wake came earnest and committed missionaries, and from their amateur scholarship, and from their notes and journals, the first anthropological study of the Māori began. A written form of their language was developed, and a greater understanding of them was promoted, albeit based on the belief that the ideal future lay in their Anglicization and conversion to Christianity.

Marsden never based himself in New Zealand, and apart from numerous visits, he remained domiciled in New South Wales. From about 1819 onwards, however, his visits to New Zealand were driven less by missionary zeal and more by a growing curiosity, as well as a deepening regard for the land and people of North Island. His journals began to be populated by vivid descriptions of his many journeys, and much technical, geographic detail. In 1820, he traveled overland from Rangihoua to Tauranga in the company of the Taiamai chief Te Morenga, returning via Kaipara on the west coast, and Whangarei on the east coast, conducting the first comprehensive geographic survey of the Northern Peninsular. He followed that up with an overland journey across the Auckland Isthmus, describing for the first time Manukau Harbor. These efforts, while partly scientific and recreational, were always underwritten by an interest in spreading the influence of the mission, and they would set the tone for similarly important missionary journeys by men such as Henry Williams, Octavius Hadfield, and most notably William Colenso.

Colenso

William Colenso was a Cornishman and cousin of John William Colenso, the Anglican Bishop of Natal. Most of the east coast of North Island was brought into scientific understanding by Colenso, who was a printer, botanist, explorer and politician, over and above his work as a missionary. He certainly would be an influential figure in the early life of the colony, but he was also one of its most passionate early naturalists, once describing the nature of the islands as "the living garment in which the Invisible has robed His mysterious loveliness." Throughout his travels, most of Colenso's journeys of exploration were primarily to locate and convert isolated Māori groups, but he also collected thousands of biological samples, marking the first orchestrated effort to catalogue and describe the unique flora and fauna of the two islands.

Besides the missionaries, the other great force for exploration was the New Zealand Company. It was responsible for quite a considerable amount of incidental exploration, undertaken as part of its overall objective to find viable lands for systematic and organized settlements. These expeditions, on the whole, were reasonably well funded, and diligently and professionally undertaken. Superficial but detailed surveying was undertaken, which allowed for mapping and some topographical details to be filled in, and it was through this work that most of the richest valleys and fertile plains were identified and claimed.

The New Zealand Company, although entirely commercial, also made some effort towards scientific survey. On the survey ship *Tory,* which arrived in the Cook Strait in 1839, there was a German physician and naturalist named Johann Karl Ernst Dieffenbach along, and he was paid a good retainer and commissioned to "explore" and report on his findings. Dieffenbach took to the mountains and forests, scaling, after two attempts, Mount Egmont (Mount Taranaki), located on the north shore of Cook Strait. This caused a great deal of consternation among the local Māori, for whom the mountain was "*tapu,*" or under "sacred occupation," and strictly off limits to people. Of course, this kind of activity made clear that the traditions and superstitions of the Māori were bound to come under assault by Anglo-Saxon Christians, but nonetheless, Dieffenbach's findings were published as *Travels in New Zealand*, which was received to great acclaim and interest all over Europe. In 1841, while still engaged with the New Zealand Company, he recorded the first European visit to Lake Rotomahana and "The Pink Terrace," or *Te Otukapuarangi*, a geothermal hot spring and at the time the largest deposit of silica sinter in the world. His description generated considerable international interest, but the site was lost in the eruption of Mount Tarawera in 1886 and only rediscovered in 2011.

Thus, by 1841, North Island was largely mapped and understood, and as far as commercial and scientific expeditions went at the time, the exploration of the North Island of New Zealand was rather an agreeable experience. It cost nothing in human life and relatively little in terms of money.

Subsequently, the New Zealand Company cast its eyes south and began to probe inland along the north coast of South Island. The first substantial landfall in this direction was made in the Bay of Tasman, where the settlement of Nelson was founded. The site seemed to be ideal for the purpose of settlement, in particular as a natural harbor, but arable land was not abundant in the hinterland. A party under the surveyor Frederick Tuckett headed north along the coast, mapping Golden Bay, while junior surveyor John Sylvanus Cotterell, leading another party at the age of 23, made his way south, finding himself eventually in the idyllic Wairau Valley.

Wairau Valley was manna to any settler. A well-drained valley, flat, sparsely forested, and with deep and fertile soils. It could quite easily have been any one of the English Shires. Cotterell hurried back and broke the news, and the attention of the Company immediately shifted in this direction. This brought about what came to be known as the "Wairau Affray," one of the first scuffles to mark the commencement of hostilities with the Māori in the area. In one particular engagement, John Sylvanus Cotterell himself was killed, at the tender age of twenty-three.

When the dust had settled and the Māori were pacified, the Company pressed southwards, sending yet another surveyor, Thomas Brunner, to follow up on reports from local Māori of a fertile inland plain somewhere in the southern interior. There, in the company of a draftsman by the name of Charles Heaphy, a man named William Fox, and a Māori guide by the name of

Kehu, Brunner discovered first Lake Rotoiti, and then nearby Lake Rotoroa, opening up another pocket of territory for future settlements. The area is certainly beautiful, but it was hard to access in the early 19th century, so it was less attractive to potential settlers.

Brunner

In March 1846, Brunner, Heaphy, and Kehu embarked on an ambitious overland expedition from Farewell Spit, at the top end of Golden Bay, south along the west coastal interior of South Island, towards the Buller River. The party was still searching for the elusive inland plain. The landscape, while still breathtaking, offered even less prospects for settlement, and eventually most of the party turned back.

In December 1846, Brunner set off without his white companions, now in the company of Kehu and one other Māori guide called Pikewate. He was neither seen nor heard from again until June 1848, when he arrived back in Tasman Bay after a journey across South Island that took 550 days. This epic journey carried him south along the west coast, then through the heart of the Southern Alps, finally reaching as far south as the mouth of the Paringa River, about two-thirds of the way down the length of South Island. There he turned inland along the Arahura River, once again entering the Southern Alps, returning eventually to Nelson after a concluding leg up the spine of the island.

This was the first major exploration likely to attract the attention of the geographic establishment in England, and it did. In 1848, Brunner published his account of the journey in a book entitled The *Great Journey: an expedition to explore the interior of the Middle Island, New Zealand.* This was greeted by the public with acclaim, and it offered the first detailed insight of the South Island interior. For this achievement, he was recognized and honored not only by the Royal Geographic Society but also the *French Société de Géographie.* The expedition has since come to be known simply as the "Great Journey."

One thing Brunner discovered was that no utopian plain awaited English herds in the interior of the island, so the search was directed elsewhere. The settler communities around Nelson, already firmly established and cramped by hill country and mountain-fringed lands, began pushing south and east. By then, there plenty of people to form parties that fanned out in all viable directions, and in 1852, stockmen Edward Lee and Edward Jollie were successful in guiding a herd of 1,800 sheep southwards along the Wairau River Valley, crossing a range of low mountains via what came to be known as Jollies Pass, and on to Hanmer. This was another seminal moment in the settlement of South Island, opening up access to the lush lowlands of the leeward slopes of North Island. Drained and sheltered by the Southern Alps, and with a north and central European climate, it was populated by few Māori, and it was earmarked for settlement almost immediately. Christchurch came into formal existence fairly soon afterwards in 1848, and by 1850, the first settlers were establishing the inland settlement of Canterbury.

With the path found and the way clear, the next challenge to face was to forge passages and find routes that could blaze a trail across the central divide from the east to the east coast. As an incentive, the government floated the very modest reward of £100 for the discovery of such a pass. If one were to consider that the bounty on the Northwest Passage stood at that time at £20,000, it certainly was not for the money that Leonard Harper, son of the first Anglican bishop of Christchurch, scouted the first viable route. In 1857, he traversed South Island from west to east, giving his name to the route that he forged, Harper Pass.

Despite claiming for its namesake the first laurels and the £100 reward, Harper Pass did not altogether satisfy the requirements of a practical route across the Southern Alps. This was achieved seven years later, in 1864, by Arthur Dobson, son of Edward Dobson, the Provincial Engineer for Canterbury Province. Arthur Dobson would later be known as Sir Arthur Dobson, having been appointed a Knight Bachelor in the 1931 New Year Honors list. He chose the route of the Waimakariri and Bealey Rivers, broaching the divide and reaching the west coast via the Ōtira River. This route became Arthur's Pass and is still one of the main routes across the central divide of South Island today.

Dobson

As an unintended consequence of his pioneering work, Arthur Dobson opened up what would be one of the main transit routes for prospectors and freebooters entering the mountainous interior once rumors of gold reached the rest of the colony. In fact, from 1860, the pattern of exploration and settlement ceased to be driven by land and became more a question of searching for minerals. This brought thousands of diggers into the foothills and mountains, and largely by this process, the minutia of this inaccessible region of the island was eventually mapped.

The first significant gold discovery was made in Otago in 1861, in the southeastern region of South Island, centered on Queenstown and on the shores of Lake Wakatipu. This brought a rush of arbitrary explorers in the southern quarter of the Southern Alps, and they established many localized routes and yet more passes west across the divide. This, in turn, resulted in the settlement by whites of the last redoubt of unclaimed land on South Island. The settlements of Dunedin and Invercargill thereafter took root, and it could reasonably be said that the best land was now taken, and settlement was complete. By then, all that remained was the occasional inaccessible valley or high mountain peak, and for the next few years, these were investigated and, if possible, settled.

All that was left was to fill in all the details, which could be done by recreational explorers. One of the first of these, and certainly the most famous, was Charles Edward Douglas. Charles Douglas was a well-born Scotsman who became eventually so synonymous with tramping the lonely reaches of the Southern Alps that he won the moniker on South Island as "Mr. Explorer Douglas." Born in 1840, he moved to New Zealand and arrived in Port Chalmers on the southeast coast in 1862. He landed on North Island but was immediately captivated by the natural splendor of the Southern Alps, and although he worked occasionally to fund his obsessive journeys into the high country, for the next few years he was almost exclusively traveling in the wilder regions of the south. Soon he established an exploration partnership and an enduring personal friendship with German surveyor Gerhard Mueller, for much of the next 40 years, the two men explored and mapped the mountainous regions of South Island.

Douglas (left) with Arthur Paul Harper

Douglas wrote no books, but he contributed numerous reports and articles to, among other publications, the "Appendix to the Journal of the House of Representatives." His sketches and watercolors, although not accomplished from an artistic standpoint, chronicled the disappearing traditions of Māori life, and he produced landscapes so fresh and imaginative that they helped capture the interest of a settler population tending to take more notice of the land and its resources than the natural splendor of their new home.

The New Zealand Wars

"They were so generous as to tell us they would come and attack us in the morning." – Captain James Cook

The years immediately following the signing of the Treaty of Waitaki were characterized by a flood of white immigration and settlement, far more than those signatories to the Treaty, and their descendants, could ever have imagined. In 1845, the tensions and anxieties erupted into a series of conflicts known as the "Māori Wars," and more recently, the "New Zealand Wars."

The question at the root of this period of New Zealand history is whether a majority of those Māori leaders who signed the Treaty of Waitaki really understood what terms they were agreeing to. Even if they did, the terms included in the treaty were vague at best, and certainly no limits were imposed on the alienation of land, and nor the numbers of immigrants expected in the colony.

At its conception, the idea of limiting the sale of Māori land to the government, thereby banning any sale between two private parties, was primarily to protect the Māori from exploitation from the many agencies, the New Zealand Company among them, with an interest in acquiring large tracts. In general, the Māori sought trade with the Europeans, and land was a tradable commodity. The Māori as a race did not quite hold the land in the manner that the Australian aboriginal did, as a commonly held natural resource, as free to all as the air or the water, and so dealing with them over the matter of land acquisition was somewhat more give and take.

Inevitably, as the pace of immigration quickened, so the government began to come under increasing pressure to make land available for agriculture and settlement. In the 1850s, an organization known as the "Māori King Movement" or *Kīngitanga,* came into being in the central region of North Island, to resist the alienation of Māori land. What set the match to the tinder was the controversial 1859 purchase by Governor Colonel Sir Thomas Gore-Browne of a disputed block of land in the Waitara district in the southwest of North Island. The Kīngitanga resisted, and loudly protested, which Governor Gore-Browne, an imperious and belligerent character, interpreted as a direct challenge to his authority. Imperial troops were brought in from the various Australian colonies, and assisted by a force of some 4,000 colonial militias and *kupapa,* which were pro-government Māori militias, the government set about provoking a war.

The New Zealand Wars occurred over a wide span of time, with the first disturbances commencing almost at the moment that the ink on the Treaty of Waitaki was dry. The first major clash, for example, took place on 17 June 1843 in the Wairau Valley of the South Island, more or less on the opposite side of the Cook Strait from the new settlements of Wellington and Nelson. The antagonist in this instance was unsurprisingly the New Zealand Company. An attempt to clear Māori from the *Ngāti Toa* tribe off land acquired by fraudulent purchase prompted a clash that resulted in the killing of twenty-two settlers and four Māori. Several more Europeans were killed after being captured. An official investigation later concluded that the settlers had been at fault, and this probably had much to do with the fact that the office of the Governor was in general hostile to the activities of the New Zealand Company. Although obviously the Company was at fault, it was unusual for blame to be so unequivocally laid at the feet of whites. Nonetheless, Governor Robert Fitzroy contemplated for a while an armed expedition to the Wairau Valley, but in the end decided against it.

This affair, known as the Wairau Affray, of the Wairau Confrontation, was the first and only armed conflict between white and Māori to take place on South Island, and some historical accounts do not place it in the general frame of the New Zealand Wars.

The more sustained conflict was triggered on North Island in March 1845, under the governorship of George Grey, a career diplomat and colonial civil servant who held known sympathies for the native subjects of the Empire. He entered almost immediately into a difficult situation as tribal leaders began mounting a strong challenge against the authority of his office. The flagstaff on a hill above Kororāreka was cut down, and a military facility burned to the ground. The leader of these disturbances was Hōne Heke, chief of the Ngāpuhi iwi, and the essential grievance was again land acquisitions, this time by the Church Missionary Society. There was by then also a widely expressed and general contempt for the terms of the Treaty of Waitaki.

The conflagration was not universally supported, and only a minority of the Ngāpuhi were in fact involved. The defeat of the small British garrison, with a minor force of local levies, at the "Battle of Ohaeawai" tended to lend the business more gravity than was perhaps justified. Nonetheless, Governor Grey, better armed and better informed than his predecessor, pursued the rebels until they were forced to sue for peace. Pragmatic terms of peace were established, and none of the leaders suffered any particular punitive measure.

Almost at the moment that hostilities died down in what later came to be known as the "Flagstaff War," renewed tension broke out in the south of North Island, as something of a sequel to the Wairau Affray, and once again, dubious land purchases and enforced removal lay at the root. Settlers were anxious to gain physical occupation of land in the valley of the Hutt River before any disputes were settled. The Hutt River drains into Wellington Harbor, and the expansion was, of course, associated with the establishment of the Wellington settlement. The same protagonists fought several engagements, with British and settler forces supported by local levies, or *kūpapa*.[10] This was a dispersed, but violent and bloody campaign, with the Māori attacking and destroying homesteads and very much taking the fight to the British. The fighting was ended by a peace settlement in 1848.

And so it continued. There were at least nine distinct wars fought between 1845 and 1872 when the New Zealand Wars were said to be officially over. The common theme of all of the individual incidences was land, land ownership, land seizure and land alienation. The initial disturbances tended to be localized, but after 1860, the scope and intensity of the conflict intensified to the extent that the government began to believe that an orchestrated and general Māori uprising was beginning to take shape. To deal with it, an appeal was made for Imperial troops, and a major and orchestrated British military campaign was mounted to neutralize the Kīngitanga, or "Māori King Movement." A secondary, and perhaps even a primary objective of this campaign, was to acquire through conquest yet more land for an ever-growing settler population.

At the height of hostilities, some 18,000 British troops were involved in operations, supported by detachments of kūpapa, and numerous ad hoc settler militias dealing with more localized equalization. The British fielded cavalry and artillery, and were opposed by a combined force of no more than 4,000 Māori warriors. The objective was obviously to once and for all crush Māori resistance, and to gain free and uninhibited access to the land.

The Māori were able to mount an effective resistance only by making use of their superior local knowledge and fluency with local conditions. The war devolved eventually into guerrilla-style conflicts that favored neither side, but which, in the end tilted in the direction of the British, simply because of superior numbers, capability and logistics. Over the course of the Taranaki and Waikato campaigns, for example, about 1,800 Māori were killed against 800 British, and total Māori losses during the combined conflict certainly exceeded 2,000, and in fact, the official Māori death toll, including civilians, was 2,154, which, out of a peak deployment of 5,000, amounted to a very heavy combined loss.

In 1863, the New Zealand Settlement Act was passed, ostensibly to formalize the chaotic events of the previous two decades, but in practical terms it simply legalized the confiscation of land as a de facto punishment for the rebellion. Land confiscation was somewhat arbitrary, directed at loyal and hostile Māori groups, and was really nothing more than a mass appropriation. More than 6,200 square miles of Māori land was seized in the aftermath of the Act. This had the additional effect of removing the main source of support and refuge for Māori rebels and holdouts.

---

[10] There were many reasons why Māori kūpapa sided with the British. In some cases it was because of genuine support for the British; in others for the sake of local and regional advantage. The use of native levies and constabularies was a mark of European colonial expansion, and a great many colonial wars were little more than civil wars.

All of this provided a basis for the end of the New Zealand Wars, and the orchestrated settlement of incoming Europeans across most of the islands. It would not be the end of the matter, however, and the legacy of land seizure and acquisition during this period remains a live issue today, and a lengthy program of reevaluation and adjustments to land ownership are ongoing today.

Upon the formal annexation of New Zealand by the British Imperial Government, the territory was established as an administrative extension of the colony of New South Wales, but by 1841, the territory existed as a colony in its own right. Its political practices and traditions, of course, were directly inherited from the British. The Crown was represented by a governor, who was advised by an appointed legislative council, and not, initially at least, a representative council. This did not take place until 1852, with the passing of the New Zealand Constitution Act, which provided for the establishment of an elected house of representatives and a legislative council. The first meeting of the General Assembly, a combined sitting of the House and Council, took place in 1854.

By this time, New Zealand was self-governing in almost every respect, with the exception of foreign affairs and defense, but also, crucially, in anything related to native affairs and native policy. This, by then, had become a reasonably common policy in British imperial administration, and much of the reason for it had to do with the fact that the Imperial Government simply did not place enough trust in its settler communities overseas to deal equally and fairly with matters of land and resources in relation to natives, tribes and peoples. In New Zealand, this would remain the case until the late 1860s, as the New Zealand Wars were tailing off, at which point the comprehensive and legal settlement of many of the associated issues began.

The provincial structure of the colony initially included three provinces, and these were New Ulster (North Island, north of the Patea River), New Munster (North Island, south of Patea River, plus South Island) and New Leinster (Stewart Island). These were amended under the New Zealand Constitution Act 1852, and six new provinces were established, namely Auckland, New Plymouth, Wellington, Nelson, Canterbury and Otago. Each was empowered with its own legislature that elected its own speaker and superintendent. The franchise was extended to anyone of twenty-one years or older, owning freehold property worth £50 or more.

Between November 1858 and December 1873, four additional provinces were introduced, and these were Hawkes Bay, Marlborough, Westland and Southland. Soon after the establishment of these new subdivisions, the whole concept of provinces was debated and eventually removed. Under the premiership of Harry Atkinson, tenth premier of New Zealand, the Abolition of Provinces Act of 1876 was passed which replaced provinces with regions.

This, then, was the constitutional character of New Zealand as the colony approached the dawn of the 20th century. The territory had been comprehensively pacified, the Māori put in their place, but the land itself remained largely unexplored and very sparsely understood. Naturalists and explorers found themselves confronted by a wild and enigmatic land, filled with exotic flora and fauna found nowhere else, and while the bloody business of claiming the land was underway, there were many other Europeans wandering the land, mapping it, exploring it and trying to understand its intricacies.

The Economics of Settlement

Before the arrival of whites on New Zealand shores, Māori trade was based on gifting and barter. This was the case in many regions of the world where British interests began to predominate, and the standard strategy to break these traditional bonds of lifestyle and economy was to impose poll taxes on individuals or households. These were intended, over and above revenue collection, to create a need for coinage, and once they had created that need, the British could force indigenous heads of households into the labor economy to earn it. A secondary benefit of this system was to create a consumer mindset, and thus provide opportunities for trade. Of course, this offered European manufacturers a steady and growing market for their goods.

In New Zealand, this did not happen because the Māori were willing to quickly adapt without forcible prompting. Goods and foodstuffs were produced for sale, and a cash economy developed among the Māori almost immediately. That said, the majority of the Māori remained on the lower rungs of the trade hierarchy and were only ever approached to sell goods in their hands, or in the settlements. For the most part, timber, fish, whales, fur seals, and other wildlife resources were simply taken without regard to their ownership or traditional usage.

The initial pillars of the New Zealand economy were whaling and fur trading, with timber following on a little later. In due course, timber exploitation expanded to the point that most viable reserves of New Zealand hardwoods were destroyed. The flax industry certainly did involve the direct participation of the Māori since the crop was grown by them on their traditional lands, but with widespread and large-scale white settlement, the traditional economy was turned on its head. The economics of timber, for example, shifted to more concentrated production involving mechanization and steam power.

All of this was transitory and amounted to primary exploitation as a means of establishing an economic foundation. There never was any real doubt that New Zealand would be founded on agriculture, and at least in the medium term, this was true. Mining would not feature in the New Zealand economy in the short to medium term, but it was gold above all, and Māori agricultural and food production that bridged the period between settlement and the development of commodity markets and the export of crops.

It was not until the 1840s that an economy in the established Western sense of the word began to take shape in New Zealand. Once again, it was the greater ballast of New South Wales that drove the process. Centered around Sydney, but with centers popping up all along the Australian coast, a vibrant local economy flourished, based on slaves or very cheap convict labor. For example, the first bank, the Union Bank of Australia, established a branch in 1840 in Petone, now a bedroom community of Wellington on the lower Hutt River. Currencies in circulation in New Zealand at the time were varied, with institutions based in Sydney tending to regulate and control the money market in New Zealand.

It was not until 1846 that the colonial government authorized the founding of the Colonial Bank of Issue. This was a rather short-lived effort to create a local, government-owned authority to issue banknotes specific to New Zealand and act as a central bank. The Colonial Bank of Issue was established by an Ordinance of the Governor of New Zealand, Sir George Grey, but in 1856, under pressure from the Colonial Parliament (and perhaps more so from the Union Bank of Australia), it was wound up. The entire effort was regarded with suspicion both in Sydney and London, seen perhaps by both as rather too independent and experimental, and it was advised in the end by the Colonial Office to cease operations.

Sir George Grey was an unusual man in the rotating constellation of colonial governors, insofar as he was liberal, deeply interested in native culture, and an original thinker. Faced with a colony that was without a tax base and depending mostly on trade levies and the sale of public land, he created a very respectable economic and social infrastructure, albeit mainly on North Island.[11] Under his administration, an infrastructure of roads, ports, railways, school and hospitals was begun, and by the 1860s, a reasonable civic structure was in place on both islands. Exploration of the islands was by then more or less complete, and public attention was turning more and more to the matter of economic development.

Again, it was gold that provided the next economic stepping stone, and the center of that economy was Dunedin in the far southwest of the colony. Gold was discovered as early as 1852 in the region of the Coromandel Peninsula, triggering a small gold rush that generated some localized prosperity, but it did not amount to a major economic boom. A far richer strike was made in 1861 in Otago, in the southeast of South Island, and this put the settlement of Dunedin on the economic map of New Zealand. The Union Bank of Australia was one of the first to establish a branch in Dunedin, but others soon followed, and between 1861 and 1870, gold comprised at least half of all New Zealand exports. In 1863, that figure was 70%. Wool and timber trailed far behind.

As is almost always true with mineral booms, the basis of the economy did not diversify when it was flush with gold. When the end came, it became clear that judicious investments had not been made, and that there was nothing to sell. The New Zealand Gold Rush, or the "Otago Gold Rush," is dated typically between 1861 and 1864, and it hardly compares to the scale of the Australian or South African gold rushes, or even the California Gold Rush. It netted a

---

[11] Readers will recall that under the terms of the Waitaki Treaty, the government held a right of preemption, and land, therefore, could only be sold to settlers by the government.

respectable sum while the going was good, but from there it did not emerge as an enduring industry, as would prove true again in Australia and South Africa.

Thus, when gold inevitably slumped in the mid-1860s, there really was nothing to take its place, and the economy slid into recession. Gum, flax, timber, grain, wool and tallow comprised less than 10% of total exports, and even gold, at the height of production, did not prevent the development of a large trade deficit. The colony was spending more than it was earning, and the shortfall was met by incoming capital. Some of it was investment capital, but the bulk was brought into the territory as life savings by the floods of new migrants.

Another unique phenomenon was that the settler population of New Zealand was scattered across a diverse region, often separated by mountain ranges and straits, so the economy of New Zealand tended to develop as a number of almost independent sub-economies flourished in practical isolation. This was a legacy of independent settlement and the fact that settlements popped up before government. The only solution to this was to create the infrastructure that would link these dispersed communities together and offer the opportunity for them to enter more deeply and more comprehensively the hinterlands of their various coastal centers. In 1863, therefore, the Provincial Government of Canterbury broke ground on the construction of the first railway line in the colony.

This set in motion a new economic phase, the main driver of which was the eighth New Zealand Premier, Sir Julius Vogel. Vogel was vibrant and dynamic, but he was also impulsive and reckless. He was the first New Zealander to write a science fiction novel, *Anno Domini 2000, or, Woman's Destiny*, which was a quirky and dystopian tale set in the year 2000, when women have come to occupy an equal role in industry, commerce, and government with men. While 21st century societies wouldn't consider that dystopian, it certainly proved somewhat prophetic, especially in New Zealand.

Vogel

Vogel established the primary economic impetus for the commencement of a centralized and coordinated system of railways. Prior to then, railway construction had taken place in isolated and disconnected pockets, using different gauges that had exemplified the fact there was no central coordination. The first railway line in Canterbury ran for just a few miles, and it was intended to service ships at the Ferrymead Wharf. It ran along a gauge of 5'3 on rolling stock imported from Australia. A few years later, in February 1867, the Southland Provincial Government opened a branch railway from Invercargill to Bluff, about 30 miles. This line, however, was built to the international standard of 4'8.

In 1870, with less than 100 miles of assorted line in the colony, Julius Vogel proposed funding national railway construction by raising foreign loans to the value of £10 million. A national gauge of 3'6 was adopted, and in 1873, the first track on North Island was completed, linking central Auckland with the town of Onehunga, a distance of about 10 miles. In 1873, the first express train from Dunedin to Christchurch was inaugurated, covering a distance of 230 miles in just 11 hours. By 1879, it became possible to travel by rail from Christchurch to Invercargill, about 380 miles. By 1880, almost 1,300 miles of railway had been completed.

In 1876, the provinces were abolished and management of the various railways came under central government control, first under the general department of public works, and later under a specific department of railways.

Vogel served two terms as Prime Minister of New Zealand, from 1873-1875 and again in 1876. The impact of that period was quite profound, in part because of his infrastructural developments, which included not only the railways but also an extensive program of roads, ports and telegraph links, all of which brought New Zealand very much into the modern global economy. According to historian Warwick R. Armstrong, author of *An Encyclopedia of New Zealand*, "He [Vogel] saw New Zealand as a potential 'Britain of the South Seas', strong both in agriculture and in industry, and inhabited by a large and flourishing population."

Vogel certainly went some way towards achieving that, and when the British Empire was plunged into recession in the late 1870s, triggering what came to be known as the "Long Depression," New Zealand was one of few emerging economies that retained positive growth.

During Britain's recession, immigration into the colony was flat for the first time in its history, and for a brief period, more whites were leaving the colony than arriving. However, with the development in the 1880s of refrigerated meat and dairy exports, an industry was founded that would remain the cornerstone of the New Zealand economy to the present day. It was then that New Zealand began to develop the reputation of "Britain's Farm," and by the eve of World War I, meat and dairy exports, mainly to Britain, made up 35% of exports, supported by wool. During World War I, due to the economics of war, imports of imperial commodities to Britain increased massively, and feeding and clothing an army absorbed as much meat, dairy, and wool possible.

The Social Landscape

Somewhat fittingly given Vogel's future vision of society in 2000, New Zealand was the first Anglophone region of the world, and the first self-governing colony, to grant the franchise to women. Indeed, the feminist movement as a whole in New Zealand was considerably more advanced than almost anywhere else in the world.

The Electoral Bill granting voting rights to women was passed in the local assembly in 1892, receiving royal assent a year later. This came about as a consequence of some two decades of vigorous campaigning, led by several prominent personalities and mainly centered around the New Zealand Chapter of the Women's Christian Temperance Union. The woman at the forefront of this struggle was Kate Sheppard, a middle-class Scotswoman who moved to New Zealand in 1863.

Sheppard

A year after the introduction into law of the 1892 Electoral Bill, a fellow Scotswoman by the name of Elizabeth Yates was elected mayor of Onehunga, making her the first female mayor to take office in any part of the British Empire. Another interesting development along these lines was the 1926 election of Margaret Magill, an open lesbian, to the Executive Board of the New Zealand Educational Institute. As women became eligible to serve at various levels in government and within the legislature, they did so. In 1919, for example, in the year that they became eligible to do so, three women stood for election to the House of Representatives.

The question of women's suffrage was just one pillar of the colonial agenda, but perhaps more important was the question of native rights and native representation. It is worth noting here that across the spectrum of the British Empire, at least according to its unwritten charter, there was a guarantee of equality for all subjects, regardless of race, color, or creed. This, it must be emphasized, lay as the central tenet of an empire seen by the British as a force for regeneration and good in a world scarred by generations of industrial slavery. In most cases, however, the various colonial administrations on the ground found ways around this, usually based on education and property qualifications. Simply put, limits were set high enough to limit indigenous access to the vote.

In South Africa, no particular effort was made to disguise what was an eventual and complete exclusion of blacks from the franchise of voting, based on the simple criteria of race. In other colonies, gerrymandering voter rights and qualifications usually succeeded in excluding blacks. In Australia, by specific legislation, Aboriginals were excluded from voting except under specific circumstances, and this remained the case until 1962.

The situation in New Zealand, however, was rather unique, and this is for the same reason that early Europeans found the Māori so much easier to deal with, trade with, and employ than Aborigines. In general, the Māori sense of social cohesion and sophistication made the concept of their direct representation in parliament easier to tolerate than introducing an Aborigine or a black African to the legislature might have at the time. Conveniently, Māori numbers in New Zealand were also small and shrinking. The Māori population suffered a cataclysm in the period after large-scale European settlement, with their numbers recorded in an 1896 census at just under 40,000, less than half of Captain Cook's estimate of 100,000 (which historians now regard as quite realistic). The numbers dwindled because of war and a steady attrition of introduced diseases, so the Māori as a whole were somewhat politically apathetic. During the early years of British administration, almost the entire Māori population remained locked into communal ownership of land, which, in and of itself, disqualified most individuals from voter registration.

Nonetheless, a debate over the question of Māori representation in the colonial legislature was ongoing. The generally high standard of white immigration created a liberal social and political environment that meant the ideal of universal suffrage was not hampered by an instinctive, class-orientated antipathy for the native population, no matter what its individual merits.

Ultimately, the wars of the 1860s brought this issue to a head. The argument was simply that Māori representation would take some of the sting out of the tectonic changes that their society experienced, and would reduce tensions between the races. If a man could not redress his grievances peacefully on the hustings, he would certainly do so armed and in the field. Others saw it simply as an opportunity to reward loyal Māori groups who had fought on the side of the Crown during the New Zealand Wars.

Thus, in 1867, a private members bill was introduced by Donald McLean to create four reserved Māori parliamentary seats. Donald McLean was a liberal, pro-Māori, and one of the most influential figures in relations between the two sides. Prior to his parliamentary career, he had served on various land committees, and eventually as Native Secretary and Land Purchase Commissioner. He was, incidentally, yet another Scotsman. The Bill was popular, and it passed through the legislature relatively easily, resulting in the Māori Representation Act of 1867. What was groundbreaking about this Act, and perhaps a little ironic, was the provisions made in the act to overcome difficulties of Māori communal land ownership. In practical terms, the only solution to this problem was universal suffrage for Māori men, which was granted. Thus, it preceded universal suffrage for white men by 12 years.[12]

These reserve seats were always intended to be temporary, lasting only five years, but it is nonetheless difficult to overstate quite how revolutionary the idea was. The equality of all British subjects was an article of faith across the British Empire, but a no less potent article of faith in the colonies themselves was to keep the natives out of active politics. These reserve seats were made permanent in 1876, mainly because of the tenacity with which a majority of Māori retained their status as communal landowners, but also because the principle simply worked.

The arrangement of these seats was unique insofar as the Māori electorates were superimposed over the white electorates, so that Māori electoral districts comprised four on North Island and one on South Island, regardless of the delineations of the common voters roll. This amounted to very limited representation, in practical terms, for universal Māori suffrage was only in respect of Māori voting for Māori representatives, while access to the common voter's role remained subject to the usual educational and property qualifications. Māoris could qualify for this in common with everyone else, but very few actually did.

Moreover, the ratio of representation was rather skewed. By population, based on the 72 white seats in parliament, the Māori qualified for between 14-16 seats. This meant that Māori representatives were allied to widely dispersed constituencies and large electorates, and pressure began to be applied to address this, but it would be more than a century before any review of the system would take place.

Initially, Māori political engagement was listless, but through the 1870s and 1880s, a greater interest began to develop. The first Māori members of parliament tended to be drawn from those tribes and clans that remained loyal to the Crown, or at least neutral during the New Zealand Wars. The 1893 Electoral Bill that conferred the right to vote on women also extended that same right to Māori women, and changes made to the law in 1893 and 1896 completed the almost absolute separation of Māori and white electoral systems. The Māori voted within their electoral system and whites in theirs, and as a population of mixed-blood members began to represent a separate political force, they were given the right to choose which electoral system they would wish to fall under.

All the while, the status of the Māori as communal landowners eventually came within the crosshairs of numerous colonial governments determined to break this monopoly. This was as much for reasons of regulating land tenure as it was reducing Māori dependence on the system. It also aimed to open up more prime land to white settlement. In the first half of the 19th century, about 8.8 million hectares of land lay under direct Māori communal occupation, a figure that was reduced by more than half by the latter 19th century, and halved again by 1900.

---

[12] Universal Male Suffrage in New Zealand entered law in 1879, and it came about largely because of the abolition of the provinces, and the centralization of power, in combination with mass immigration and economic depression.

New Zealand at War

"Truly the early settlers in a new colony do become extraordinary beings, somewhat, I imagine, of the Kentucky style, half horse, half alligator, with a touch of earthquake"– Sarah Mathew, diarist (1841)

As the end of the 19th century loomed, the British Empire reached the greatest extent of its geographic scope. Odd territories would be added here and there, but for the most part the process was complete. The main territorial components of the British Empire were India, Canada, Australia, New Zealand and South Africa. South Africa, however, was complex because it comprised two independent Boer republics and two British colonies, and tensions were heavy in the area. Moreover, South Africa comprised a region of vital strategic importance in the form of the Cape Peninsular, which potentially controlled shipping between the Atlantic and Indian Oceans. This lay under British control, but the Germans were just across the border in German South West Africa (the future Namibia), and if they allied with the Boer, they might conceivably oust the British from the region and declare the entire African subcontinent German. In view of the pending European war, which was daily looking more inevitable, any sign of German ambitions in that direction needed to be urgently checked, and the only way to achieve this was to place the entire region under direct British control.

There was another complicating factor too: the existence of gold and diamonds. By the last decade of the 19th century, South Africa was the largest producer of both, and the region as a whole was of pivotal economic importance to Britain. If strategic considerations were not enough to provoke a war, then the sheer weight of British investment in the region certainly would.

War was inevitable, and in October 1899, the conflict between the Boer Republics and British Empire began in earnest. The Anglo-Boer War was rather unique insofar as it deviated from the British preference for set-piece battles on predetermined battlefields. Instead, the sides engaged in a wide-ranging and mobile guerilla conflict that better suited the mounted infantry units from Australia and New Zealand.

At the start of the conflict, small British garrisons were frequently overwhelmed by a rapid Boer mobilization, and three sieges were effectively put in place until the British could begin landing a large expeditionary force.

All of the major regions of the British Empire contributed manpower to this war effort, but besides local and imperial forces, the largest overseas contingents were contributed by Australia and New Zealand. In total, New Zealand contributed 10 contingents. The first, known as the "First New Zealand Mounted Rifles," numbered 215 and departed Wellington on October 21, 1899, less than a fortnight after the outbreak of the war. It was absorbed immediately upon arrival in Cape Town into the British Expeditionary Force under the command of General

French, and deployed largely in the Orange Free State as the fortunes of war tilted very much against the British.

Four months later, as the British experienced a series of early defeats, a second contingent of 266 men was dispatched. These were drawn from a mixture of Colonial Defense Force Regulars and civilian volunteers with a particular aptitude for riding and shooting. It was becoming clear that the style of warfare under evolution in South Africa was different to anything the great British Army had ever faced before.[13] The set formations and battlefield contests of past wars now gave way to mobile guerrilla warfare that required a very different type of soldier, and both Australian and New Zealand forces proved themselves to be ideally adapted. Local contingents then began to form, with the third New Zealand contingent raised in Christchurch, the fourth and fifth from Lyttleton (now part of Christchurch), the sixth from Auckland, and so on.

The character of the Anglo-Boer War went in two phases. The first was somewhat conventional insofar as the British, caught somewhat on the back foot, were pushed into a series of sieges that held for several months before the accumulation of Imperial forces in South Africa was sufficient to begin pushing back. The sieges were then soon broken, and the Boer retreated back on their capitals of Bloemfontein and Pretoria. By the middle of 1900, both had fallen and were in British hands.

At that point, however, far from surrendering, the Boer simply abandoned the cities and took to the countryside, where a wide-ranging guerrilla campaign occupied British troops. The strategy was simply to conduct vast infantry sweeps, scorch the earth, and use mobile reconnaissance, the latter of which was where Australians and New Zealanders found their particular niche.

Part of the scorched earth policy, which was deeply controversial, was to isolate Boer women and children from their rural homesteads, thus denying the fighting commandos access to support. The British made the first comprehensive military use of concentration camps, and these camps began to generate humanitarian concern, in particular among an increasing empowered group of female humanitarian and political activists. Although there was no shortage of these in South Africa (the writer and feminist Olive Schreiner perhaps being the most famous), women from all over the British Empire volunteered to provide relief and support to Boer families languishing in camps that were poorly managed by the British military authorities. Many of these were among the first generation of trained New Zealand nurses, taking over from an amateur corps of medical assistants who had to date played the role of nurses. These women were trained under British medical instructors as part of a general professionalization of the medical system in the colony, and an exchange of personnel with Britain. While some were sponsored by the government, many made their way to South Africa on private subscriptions, or through the efforts of public fundraising. The reason for this, however, was less a matter of patriotism than humanitarianism, and it reflected the rise of the international humanitarian movement which at

---

[13] The Colonial Defence Force was active from 1862.

that moment was finding expression in all of the major imperial capitals. It was also an assertion of the progressive attitudes and social conditions of New Zealand, the only territory in the world where women enjoyed full rights of suffrage.

While New Zealand nurses dealt with the sick and dying in the camps and on the front lines, a contingent of New Zealand teachers, the "Learned Eleventh," made their way to South Africa. The New Zealand Education Act of 1877 granted the right of free education for all, which laid the bedrock of an extraordinarily progressive education system very early on in the life of the colony. By the 1890s, female teachers outnumbered men, and a sense of both adventure and empowerment inspired them. A contingent of 20 women left for South Africa on May 4, 1902, just a few weeks before the war ended. In the end, they found themselves engaged in the British reconstruction effort, teaching Boer children English in preparation for a British takeover and their absorption into the British Empire.

New Zealand as a Dominion

"Somewhere between the landing at Anzac and the end of the battle of the Somme, New Zealand very definitely became a nation." Ormond Burton, a veteran who fought at the Battle of Gallipoli

One of the first actions taken by the government of New Zealand in the 20th century was the annexation of the Cook Islands and a handful of other territories. In 1888, the Cook Islands were absorbed into the British Empire as a protectorate, and in 1901, the islands were officially handed over to New Zealand as the first colony attached to the territory. This was agreed to by the British in part as compensation for the loss of the Island of Samoa, ceded by the British in 1899 to the United States and Germany at a point when it would have seemed natural to hand administration of the islands over to New Zealand.

Thus, on June 11, 1901, the territorial extent of New Zealand was extended to cover not only Rarotonga, Aitutaki, and the remainder of the southern Cook Islands, but also the northern Cook Islands and Niue. Soon afterwards, Suwarrow and Nassau Islands were added to the Cook Islands territory. In due course, the islands of Tokelau and Naru would follow.

1901 also saw the establishment of the Commonwealth of Australia. This was a seminal moment in the history of Australia and the British Empire, for it created a significant federal dominion out of a conglomeration of ideologically aligned, but politically separate colonies. A cautiously drafted constitution created a federation with characteristics borrowed from the British, Canadian, and American federal systems, under generous terms of independence from Britain. Tasmania was part of the Australian Commonwealth, and there seemed at the time to be a natural gravitational pull attracting New Zealand into the same political union. Since the 1860s, New Zealand had been a regular attendee at Australian inter-territorial conferences, and there certainly seemed to be an organic movement towards a closer union, if not a de facto federation.

For several years the matter remained on the table, and both sides gave it a great deal of thought, but in the end, a commission of inquiry was authorized to look into the matter and concluded that a union with Australia would be incompatible with the development of New Zealand. It is also probably true that New Zealand Prime Minister Richard Seddon found the idea of leading a separate colony, soon to be a dominion, more attractive than a mere federal constituent territory.

Opinion on the matter was not unanimous, but a sense of separation between the two regions was inescapable, and part of that had to do with each population's images of themselves and the other side. The settler population of New Zealand did not descend from convicts, and New Zealanders perceived themselves superior to Australians and did not necessarily court too close an association. Furthermore, the bulk of New Zealand's export trade was to Britain, making Australia more of a rival in trade than a natural ally. In the end, the two territories were deemed too intrinsically separate for there to be a closer union.

As if to underline that fact, in 1902, the government of New Zealand established the finished form of its national flag. In the Colonial Naval Defense Act of 1865, the British government decreed that all ships owned by colonial governments must fly the Blue Ensign with the badge of the colony on it. At that time, New Zealand owned no colonial emblem as such, so it flew the Blue Ensign without a distinguishing badge. In 1866, two government ships, the *St. Kilda* and *Sturt*, were reprimanded for this practice, which caused some embarrassment and prompted the government of New Zealand to try devising a national emblem. Numerous ideas were discussed, including simply the name "New Zealand," and also the four stars of the Southern Cross, but this was rejected for reasons of its not being exclusively representative of New Zealand. For a long time the initials "NZ" were attached to the ensign for want of anything else. In 1869, however, finding this inadequate, the four stars of the Southern Cross were re-examined and then placed on the standard blue ensign in red, with a white border.

This was officially for use in maritime identification only, but it soon became the representative flag of the colony, even though the Union Jack, the flag of the British Empire, remained the legal flag of all British colonies. In 1899, a signaling flag was introduced into the Royal Navy and international Code of Signals, which meant that the flag flying over government buildings in New Zealand was suddenly flying signals and thus had to be removed. This was also at about the time that New Zealand was sending contingents of troops to South Africa, and street parades and quayside farewells were a confusing affair without a recognizable New Zealand national flag to wave. This set minds to work once again, and yet more thought was given to the question of a national flag.

The response of the government, under Prime Minister Seddon, was to introduce a New Zealand Ensign Bill in 1900 to formalize the adoption of the Blue Ensign with the stars of the Southern Cross in red, bordered with white the legal flag of New Zealand. The Bill required some modification, however, because flying the Blue Ensign was, after all, a Royal Navy prerogative, and its use for all and sundry under New Zealand jurisdiction offended the Admiralty's sense of exclusivity. A second bill was therefore introduced in 1901 and was passed in November of that year. It was approved by the Crown a few months later, and the news was published in the *New Zealand Gazette* on June 27, 1902.

The next major political milestone was the award of dominion status to New Zealand, which took place on September 26, 1907. The question of what the word "Dominion" actually means is unlikely to ever be answered in the same way twice, but in the British Empire's hierarchy, standards of recognition ranged from a simple "sphere of influence" to a "protectorate," a "colony," a "self-governing colony," and a "dominion." The word "dominion" came into use in about 1867 because of America's disapproval of the term "kingdom" in regards to the drafting of the "Constitution Act," or the "British North America Act," of that same year, which created "one dominion under the name of Canada." The term "dominion" then came to imply something closer to an independent sovereignty than the word "colony," which had hitherto described every British overseas territory from a speck in the South Pacific to the vast extent of Canada. As the key English-speaking colonies matured to the extent that they effectively ran themselves and were no longer answerable in any real sense to Whitehall, a more loosely defined imperial federation, or commonwealth, began to replace the centralized imperial structure of yore. Numerous colonies around the world, primarily in what might today be regarded as the "developing world," remained under direct rule, but entities such as Canada, Australia, New Zealand, and South Africa certainly did not. The formalization of dominion status, therefore, marked something of a coming of age.

As part of the new dispensation between Britain and her overseas territories was the convening of regular imperial conferences, whereby the various prime ministers of the self-governing regions met, usually in London, and there, affairs of the empire were discussed. In 1901, Australia became a "dominion" with the advent of the Australian Federation although it referred to itself as a "Commonwealth."

It was during the Empire Conference of 1907 that the question of New Zealand's formal elevation to the status of "dominion" came under discussion. Prime Minister Joseph Ward put it to the imperial authorities that New Zealand had outgrown the designation of "colony," and was as much deserving of the title "dominion" as Australia and Canada.[14] This was also an expression of regional imperial ambitions on the part of New Zealand, which had by then begun to regard itself as wholly separate from Australia, and heir to a leadership role in the South Pacific. The Order in Council altering the title of the territory from "colony" to "dominion" was issued on September 9, and the proclamation was made the next day, taking effect on September 26, 1907.

In terms of constitutional changes, there were none. An attempt was made to proclaim a

---

[14] South Africa would not become a dominion until the four separate colonies were united in 1910.

"Dominion Day," but this never caught on, and all that really changed was that the term "Premier" in describing the local leadership changed to "Prime Minister" although the two terms had already been interchangeable since the establishment of that post.

As for independence from Britain, while a majority celebrated the adoption of the term "dominion," few desired any practical separation from Britain. The ties of kinship remained very strong, trade interests were strong, and a sense of belonging was absolute, a fact that would be reinforced by the bonds of common defense during World War I and World War II.

Indeed, when the United Kingdom declared war on Germany in 1914, the government of New Zealand was not wholly and immediately committed to Britain's defense, but the general public of New Zealand responded immediately. Out of a population of approximately 1.1 million at the time, almost 100,000 New Zealanders served the Allied Powers in the war, and among them were almost 2,200 Māori and some 500 Pacific Islanders. 11 Victoria Crosses were won by New Zealand soldiers, with a further 5 won by New Zealanders serving either with Australian or British forces. Some 18,000 died, and over 41,000 were injured or incapacitated. Of these, 2,779 died at Gallipoli and more than 12,000 on the Western Front.

Gallipoli is often regarded as the battle that helped form a separate national identity for both New Zealand and Australia. By the end of 1914, the Allied Powers were seriously worried. The Western Front had bogged down into trench warfare, Russia had been badly mauled on the Eastern Front, and in October of 1914, the Ottoman Empire had joined the war on the side of the Central Powers. For a century, the West had considered the Ottoman Empire the "sick man of Europe." Bogged down with corruption and inefficient bureaucracy, and riven by sectarian strife, what was once one of the greatest empires in history seemed ready to fall apart, yet it was still a serious foe. It commanded a vast manpower and rich resources, as well as territory stretching from the Balkans to the Persian Gulf. Most critically, it controlled the Dardanelles, the narrow, 38-mile long strait connecting the Aegean Sea to the Sea of Marmora. At the northeastern end of the Sea of Marmora lay the Ottoman capital of Istanbul, now Istanbul, and a narrow channel, called the Bosporus, leading to the Black Sea. Gallipoli is the hilly peninsula of land along the north coast of the Dardanelles on the European side, while the south coast is on the Asian side. Dominated on both sides by high ground, no ship was able to pass through the straits unscathed without Ottoman permission. Russia had been cut off from her allies to the west, Britain and France needed Russia's grain, and Russia desperately needed Western supplies and munitions.

Early in the war, the Ottomans knew the Dardanelles strait would most certainly be attacked and had prepared significant defenses. The plan drafted by the then First Lord of the Admiralty, Winston Churchill, was meant to destroy Ottoman defenses along the Dardanelles. However, Allied forces comprised of British, Irish, Australian and New Zealand troops were unable to penetrate the Ottoman defenses, advancing only about 100 meters from the shores. The Ottomans, led by German General Liman von Sanders, further reinforced their positions. The later attempt of the British to establish a new beachhead was more successful, yet the British government refused to send significant reinforcements.

In December 1915, what was certainly the most successful part of the Gallipoli offensive, the evacuation of the British forces, began. Only two men were wounded in the entire operation, and the Turks hadn't suspected a thing until the last man had long gone. Still, the Gallipoli Campaign was one of the most defining battles in the military history of both New Zealand and Australia, and of the 44,000 Allied casualties sustained in the campaign, 8,700 were Australian and 2,779 were Kiwi. For two dominions with such comparatively tiny populations, losses on this scale were keenly felt. For the Turks too, victory, if that is a correct description, came at a high price, as Ottoman casualties were estimated at 87,000.

A minor legacy of World War I was the commencement of a tradition of calling New Zealanders "Kiwis," a name which was given to them as a term of endearment by other Allied troops, and which they then adopted.

Word War I knocked four major global empires out of the international picture, and their departure altered the global dynamic significantly. The League of Nations was founded to deal with the necessary revision of sovereignty and rule in many liberated territories, and in some respects to replace the global empire with a world government.

It also meant the coming of age for all of the British overseas dominions, including India, and a reevaluation of the imperial relationship with Britain. The Imperial Conferences of 1917-18 were, therefore, the most important of the century to date. Much of what took place had to do with the coordination of all the imperial partners in the war under the aegis of a combined War Cabinet. The various dominions' leaders were each aware of how their engagement in the war as virtual equal partners would affect their own constitutions and political status. In April 1917, the conference passed Resolution IX, which committed all parties to a further conference after the war in order to reconfigure the imperial relationship "based upon a full recognition of the Dominions as autonomous nations of an Imperial Commonwealth."

This was an important moment in the evolution of the British Empire, simply because it marked the first official use of the term "Commonwealth." It also sounded the death knell of the British Empire. India was included in this general agreement to grant greater powers of internal decision making, in particular in regards to defense, foreign affairs, and foreign policy.

As it turned out, this did not take place immediately after World War I, and for the time being the interactions between the dominion governments of Australia and New Zealand and the British tended to focus more on regional strategic issues, such as a renewal of the Anglo-Japanese Alliance and the inclusion of India in the closed circle of British overseas dominions. India, however, remained a colony and not a dominion, which meant it was represented not by Indians, but by British cabinet officials responsible for India.[15] During the 1923 Empire

Conference, an attempt was made to forge a common, empire-wide foreign policy, but this was defeated by the leaders of South Africa and Canada, who argued that this would encroach on the autonomy of individual dominions.

It was not until the Conference of 1926 that a definitive statement on the independence of the dominions was made. This was the Balfour Declaration, named after ex-Prime Minister and Lord President of the Council Arthur Balfour, who, as chairman of the "Inter-Imperial Relations Committee," was responsible for drafting the document.[16] The key paragraph in this document declared the United Kingdom and the Dominions to be *"autonomous Communities within the British Empire, equal in status, in no way subordinate one to another in any aspect of their domestic or external affairs, though united by a common allegiance to the Crown, and freely associated as members of the British Commonwealth of Nations."* The declaration was unanimously approved by all of the various prime ministers on November 15, 1926. It was now acknowledged that the various governors and governors-general, who acted as viceroys or representatives of the Crown, would no longer automatically act as a representative of the British government in matters affecting foreign diplomatic relations. In the years to follow, British governors were gradually replaced by High Commissioners whose duties and functions echoed those of an ambassador.

These findings and conclusions were restated and confirmed in the Empire Conference of 1930 and submitted to the defining "Statute of Westminster" in 1931. This was an act of the British Parliament whereby His Majesty's Government and Parliament renounced any legislative authority over dominion affairs. Passed on December 11, 1931, the act came into effect either immediately, or upon ratification. It is interesting, however, that New Zealand did not immediately ratify the Statute of Westminster, nor, for that matter, did Australia. The issue at the heart of this was whether New Zealand really wanted full and complete independence from Britain. This was much the same sentiment that underscored a rather lackluster public response to the declaration of dominion status, and the inability of the government to interest the population in celebrating Dominion Day. New Zealand's leader at the time, Gordon Coates, referred to the Balfour Declaration more than once as a "poisonous document."

That said, on a practical level, the country behaved in all respects as if the Statute had been ratified, even if stepping into the realm of constitutional independence proved a very difficult step. It would not take place until after the end of World War II; in 1947, the Parliament of New Zealand would finally adopt the Statue of Westminster, after joining the United Nations without the title of "Dominion." New Zealand citizenship, as separate from British citizenship, came into being in 1949, at which point New Zealand effectively ceased to be a member of the British

---

[15] India was only granted dominion status after WWII. It was generally acknowledged that, like Ireland, at the moment that India was granted any degree of local autonomy, it would vote itself out of the Empire.

[16] The Balfour Declaration of 1926 should not be confused with the Balfour declaration of 1917 which recognized the right of Palestinian Jews to a homeland in the mandated territory of Palestine.

Empire.

Notwithstanding the Statute of Westminster and a loosening of the bonds of imperial kinship, all of the dominions committed themselves wholly and completely to the Allies during World War II. The Kiwis fought on land, in the air, and on the water in every theater, from North Africa to the Pacific. At the outbreak of the war, the population of New Zealand was about 1,600,000, and 140,000 Kiwis served, with 11,928 killed according to figures available from the Commonwealth War Graves Commission. Despite the fact that it had yet to ratify the Statute of Westminster, New Zealand acted independently by declaring war on Germany as a separate declaration to the British. Australia, on the other hand, maintained that the King's declaration obliged all of the dominions automatically.

The only other notable political events involving New Zealand in the run-up to 1947 was the signing in January 1944 of the Canberra Pact, a treaty of cooperation with Australia. Although it was not a formal military pact, it signaled a loose regional alliance in a post-war world. In the same vein, New Zealand joined the United Nations as a formative member in 1945.

Appendix: The Treaty of Waitangi

HER MAJESTY VICTORIA Queen of the United Kingdom of Great Britain and Ireland regarding with Her Royal Favor the Native Chiefs and Tribes of New Zealand and anxious to protect their just Rights and Property and to secure to them the enjoyment of Peace and Good Order has deemed it necessary in consequence of the great number of Her Majesty's Subjects who have already settled in New Zealand and the rapid extension of Emigration both from Europe and Australia which is still in progress to constitute and appoint a functionary properly authorized to treat with the Aborigines of New Zealand for the recognition of Her Majesty's Sovereign authority over the whole or any part of those islands – Her Majesty therefore being desirous to establish a settled form of Civil Government with a view to avert the evil consequences which must result from the absence of the necessary Laws and Institutions alike to the native population and to Her subjects has been graciously pleased to empower and to authorize me William Hobson a Captain in Her Majesty's Royal Navy Consul and Lieutenant-Governor of such parts of New Zealand as may be or hereafter shall be ceded to her Majesty to invite the confederated and independent Chiefs of New Zealand to concur in the following Articles and Conditions.

Article the first [Article 1] The Chiefs of the Confederation of the United Tribes of New Zealand and the separate and independent Chiefs who have not become members of the Confederation cede to Her Majesty the Queen of England absolutely and without reservation all the rights and powers of Sovereignty which the said Confederation or Individual Chiefs respectively exercise or possess, or may be supposed to exercise or to possess over their respective Territories as the sole sovereigns thereof.

Article the second [Article 2] Her Majesty the Queen of England confirms and guarantees to the Chiefs and Tribes of New Zealand and to the respective families and individuals thereof the full exclusive and undisturbed possession of their Lands and Estates Forests Fisheries and other properties which they may collectively or individually possess so long as it is their wish and desire to retain the same in their possession; but the Chiefs of the United Tribes and the individual Chiefs yield to Her Majesty the exclusive right of Preemption over such lands as the proprietors thereof may be disposed to alienate at such prices as may be agreed upon between the respective Proprietors and persons appointed by Her Majesty to treat with them in that behalf.

Article the third [Article 3] In consideration thereof Her Majesty the Queen of England extends to the Natives of New Zealand Her royal protection and imparts to them all the Rights and Privileges of British Subjects.

(signed) William Hobson, Lieutenant-Governor.

Now therefore We the Chiefs of the Confederation of the United Tribes of New Zealand being assembled in Congress at Victoria in Waitangi and We the Separate and Independent Chiefs of New Zealand claiming authority over the Tribes and Territories which are specified after our respective names, having been made fully to understand the Provisions of the foregoing Treaty, accept and enter into the same in the full spirit and meaning thereof in witness of which we have attached our signatures or marks at the places and the dates respectively specified. Done at Waitangi this Sixth day of February in the year of Our Lord one thousand eight hundred and forty.

Online Resources

Other British history titles by Charles River Editors

Other titles about New Zealand on Amazon

Bibliography

James Belich, Making Peoples: A History of the New Zealanders from the Polynesian settlement to the end of the nineteenth century (1996)

James Belich, Paradise Reforged: A History of the New Zealanders from 1880 to the Year 2000 (2001).

Giselle Byrnes, ed. (2009). The New Oxford History of New Zealand. Oxford University Press.

Michael King (2003) The Penguin History of New Zealand.

Leveridge, Steven. "Another Great War? New Zealand interpretations of the First World War towards and into the Second World War" First World War Studies (2016) 7#3:303-25.

Parsons, Gwen. "The New Zealand Home Front during World War One and World War Two." History Compass 11.6 (2013): 419-428.

Smith, Philippa Mein. A Concise History of New Zealand (Cambridge Concise Histories) (2nd ed. 2012)

Keith Sinclair, ed., (1996) The Oxford Illustrated History of New Zealand.

Keith Sinclair, A History of New Zealand.

Ranginui Walker (2004), Ka Whawhai Tonu Matou: Struggle Without End.

Free Books by Charles River Editors

We have brand new titles available for free most days of the week. To see which of our titles are currently free, click on this link.

Discounted Books by Charles River Editors

We have titles at a discount price of just 99 cents everyday. To see which of our titles are currently 99 cents, click on this link.

Printed in Great Britain
by Amazon